POISON
IN THE POT

VOLUME V

PASTOR DON R. VINING

ISBN 978-1-969865-46-6 (Paperback)
ISBN 978-1-969865-47-3 (Ebook)

Inquiries and Book Orders should be addressed to:
Leavitt Peak Press
17901 Pioneer Blvd Ste L #298,
Artesia, California 90701
Phone #: 2092191548

Contents

Acknowledgements

My thanks to Connie Neumann for a job well done in taking hundreds of pages of notes and capturing the message of Poison as the Pot. I believe it will bring life changes to every reader.

My heartfelt thanks to Brenda Ammons for her many hours of research and typing on this project. Without her, this project would not be complete. My appreciation to Kay Dunn, Sun Scott and Dan Williams for proofreading.

My gratitude to Dr. Carol Bartholomew for another outstanding cover design that flows with the subject of this project.

Foreword

There is a constant struggle between the spirit and the flesh. The closer to the Lord's coming, the greater the battle will be. That is why it is so vitally important that we recognize and eliminate things in our lives that distract us.

Satan is good at blinding our eyes toward situations in our lives which need to be dealt with. That is one of his greatest tactics in the world today. Our spiritual enemy has come to steal, kill and destroy all that is good.

As with former publications, in his latest book, Poison in the Pot, Pastor Don R. Vining comes across with a powerful revelation and exposes areas that need to be "cleaned up" in our lives. Poison in the Pot is a MUST read. There are parts of our lives that we never consider poisonous. There was a time in my own life when I was bitter in my heart-I never realized how Satan had slipped in so cunningly. I finally understood if I wanted more God, if I wanted Him to use me, I had to let Him have control and eliminate the poison.

Though we may fall short in how and what we are to become, there is still grace and mercy that follows us. There is a remedy for the poison in our lives. We must put more of God in than of self. Paul once said, "I must decrease so that He might increase. When we allow the Holy Spirit to deal with us on a one on one basis we give Him full authority to cleanse us and to reveal what is wrong in our lives.

My prayer is, as you read through the pages of Poison in the Pot, as I did, that God will begin to talk to you as only He can. Then, you can submit to Him whole heartily, without reservation. Allow Him to show you the poison in your life, knowing with love, He will help you remove the stuff that doesn't belong. And together, as the body of Christ, let us be all that God intends us to be in this world full of darkness.

Introduction

Change begins with awareness. If we don't know there is a problem, we certainly can't fix it. Many of the poisons floating in our lives are so subtle, and have seeped in so gradually, we aren't even aware of their presence. This book spotlights the problem areas so we can take practical steps to rid our lives of sneaky toxins.

The focus of this book is more narrow than the previous three and speaks especially to the Pentecostal movement in general, and to Pentecostals in particular. But the truths uncovered apply to every Christian, from every denomination. We all have blind spots and need to see through the muck in our lives to the poisons floating just below the surface. This book will help do that.

But, it doesn't stop there. After awareness, we must make choices. I hope the illustrations and biblical insights offered here will help you work hard and make changes to clean up the pot of your life. God's Word contains the antidote, but it won't help if we don't use it. Join me to get the poison out.

-Pastor Don R. Vining,
Belleview FL.

CHAPTER ONE

UNCOVERING THE POISON IN THE POT

Poison can be tricky stuff. Webster's Dictionary defines it as a substance that causes injury, illness, or death, especially by chemical means." But, not all poison is easy to spot. Some kinds have no color, others have no obvious smell. Some work fast; others take a long time before you notice anything different. So how do you protect yourself and your family? Through education. You read labels and obey warnings and store potential poisons out of reach of children.

I believe there is some poison that has crept into our churches and our lives-some of it so gradually, we've barely noticed it eating away our spiritual strength. We know something is wrong in our hearts, but we aren't sure what the problem is. It is time to uncover the poison in our lives and hearts. But, if you are not ready to examine the poison floating in your pot, you have wasted a trip to the bookstore, and you may want to set this book aside for a while.

The truth is, the Lord is coming back for His church. But He is not coming back for a church that has been waxed over and become calloused. The Lord is coming back for a distinctly different-looking,

1

different-acting, different-responding part of His creation. That is what He calls the true church, the church without spots or blemishes.

For too long, the church has looked like the world. For too long, our churches have preached a gospel that makes people "feel" good about serving the Lord, but never really leads them into a deeper relationship with Him.

BEGINNING WITH PASSION

The Church of God organization began some 128 years ago when a group of people set themselves apart from the ways of the world and began to seek God with passion. They probably didn't go to church with the idea that they were going to begin at 10:30a.m. and go home at 12:30p.m. sharp. They came in with the attitude that they might be accepted or might not, but it didn't matter. The organization began when a group of individuals came together and said, "God, we are ready for you to show yourself to us." The Holy Spirit was poured out on that particular group and 128 years later, the power of the Holy Spirit is still moving.

The Church of God is one of the fastest growing organizations in the world, and the fastest growing Pentecostal organization. I am excited to be part of it, but I am concerned too. Though we may be the fastest growing, that may not be enough. Out in the world, all you have to do is announce certain rock groups and thousands flock to their concert. I'm not really sure we have done everything we can do neighborhoods to reach people with the gospel. We have name recognition and the Spirit of God is being poured out, but there are t seats in our churches.

THE EDUCATED SHOUT

As much as I want to celebrate the growth of the Pentecostal movement I also want to call our attention to the fact that we may have missed some things along the way Pentecostals like the shout but what is the shouting about the shout means we are celebrating something we've learned too often there is a whole lot of shouting without true understanding.

I love to shout. I'll jump the chairs but I want to have a reason to jump I want to build a different kind of mystery when people come into our church I don't want them to feel good about sin I want the kind of ministry the kind of spirit of God that we had in our church one Wednesday afternoon.

A group of ladies decided to stay and backs in the presence of the Lord and while one was thinking she heard noises in the building another lady was thinking *it sounds just like an angel's in he*re. No sooner had the thought it then another lady spoke up and said, "Oh, the angels of the Lord are in the room in this room."

What it means is we need the kind of churches where if it is takes all day for God to touch heal deliver free and restore his people then we must say, "Okay God, let it take all day" we can't have that kind of spirit and attitude until we get into the word and understand we may be misguided in some areas.

Second Kings 4:38-41 says,

> *And Elisha came again to Gilgal; and (there was] a dearth in the land; and the sons of the prophets [were] sitting before him: and he said unto his servant, Set on the great pot, and seethe pottage for the sons of the prophets. And one went out into the field to gather herbs, and found a wild vine, and gathered thereof wild gourds his lap full, and came and shred [them] into the pot of pottage: for they knew (them) not. So they poured out for the men to eat. And it came to pass, as they were eating of the pottage, that they cried out, and said, O (thou) man of God, (there is) death in the pot. And they could not eat [thereof). But he said, Then bring meal. And he cast [it] into the pot; and he said, pour out for the people, that they may eat. And there was no harm in the pot.*

At first, there was poison in the pot. Not only poison; there was death in the pot. Now, in the Word, pottage means soup. Depending on where you are spiritually, in your mind, pottage can be the stuff that comes from the south end of a north bound mule, or it can be poison in the soup. It doesn't matter; it is all bad. It will mess you up if you eat it.

I've had people ask, "Pastor, why aren't you more modest in the things you say?" Because, I believe God has sent people who need to get down and dirty to tell it the way it is. We have been tanned and blistered with the Almighty's Word, but we are unchanged. I am ready for a change. I am

Ready to get down and dirty, to spell out what's wrong. The truth of the matter: 90% of what we allow in our life is pure garbage. We spend too much time dealing with pure slop. I want the truth of the Word to come out. The servant thought he was adding herbs-instead, he was adding wild gourds.

TAMING THE WILD VINES

There are many wild vines and gourds in the House of God. There is a lot of slop that I believe God wants us to dig through. Through His Word, God wants to show us how to do that. According to the Biblical Illustrator, "The sons of the prophets knew little the harmful quality of the food that was being poured in the pot. In all things, nature has its poisonous side as well as its sustaining and comforting aspect. The vain and the antidote are both before us in nature. In other words, in the garden, death lies very near to life. Even our most natural passions lie but a single step from their destructive application."

Think about it. Is it possible the servant went out to gather food for a natural appetite and came back with poison? Is it possible that we could go to our churches for good spiritual food and go home poisoned? Is it possible that we, in total innocence, could go to the grocery store and come home with poison?

A few months ago, my wife and I bought some crackers and other things that we needed in the house, like honey buns and sweet cakes and good midnight snacks. We also bought a jog of milk. The milk was sealed, but we learned that if something is sealed, it doesn't mean it is good. The milk sat m the refrigerator for two or three days, which was miracle in itself. I opened the jug and poured a nice tall glass to drink with my Oren cookies. After a swing. I discovered lather would have casted better. I took the milk back to the store. The manager argued with me-I should have checked the date. The date was good, so I asked, "What should I do next time? Unseal it, take the lid off and smell it before I bring it home?" She still didn't believe we had bad milk from her store, so I said, "Just take one deep breath." I convinced that precious lady to place her nose over the small rim of that jug. She did, and she almost passed out. We brought milk into the house only to find we had poison.

How often have children taken drugs thinking they were taking an aspirin? Three years ago my wife had a migraine headache, one of the ladies of the church said, "Here is some aspirin for you. Later on, while in a restaurant, my wife leaned over and said, "I am going to pass out." I knew there was a problem. The lady had given her two nerve pills.

Another time, during a camping trip, we had forgotten to buy tomatoes and cucumbers for the salad. We pulled off at a roadside stand and bought some. At the camp, once we had cut the cucumbers, we discovered they would have done better at the city dump. We went to buy something good, but ended up with something bad.

SNIFFING OUT POISON

My family makes fun of me because I always smell my food. I tell our congregation, if they invite me over for dinner, they should not take offense when I sniff my food before 1 eat it. I'm confirming there is no poison in the pot.

A few years ago, I was in dire straits for a miracle. I was very sick. A member of our church brought me some home-made soup and said, "This will cure you. I tasted it and thought animals wouldn't even eat this, but tried it out on the horses across the field. They never came back to eat over our fence again, so something must have happened.

Another time we were at a fast food restaurant. I took a bite of my taco and started sniffing. My wife said, "What is wrong? You are always sniffing." I said, "Something is wrong." God helped me sniff out bad lettuce. They had a whole bad batch in the back. We go to get good things, but that isn't always what we receive.

We go to church for good things, but if we are not careful and don't bring our notepads and Bible the Sword-to confirm the man of God is feeding us good, solid Word, we may miss it. I am tired of the kind of gospel that I have to reach for. I am ready for the kind of gospel that I can apply to my life now, because I have problems now, not in the future. I need to feel God in my life today, not next year. Thank God for the prophetic Word that He sometimes gives through an interpreter that says, "If you do this, I'll do that. I love the Word that says, "Because you have been obedient, now I am taking the time element away. That was a prophetic word, given in one of our services.

CONSIDER THE RESULTS

We don't have to earn God's blessings. He already gave His life; it was a free gift. He gave His Son at Calvary for us so we could have life. He also gave us the spirit of discernment, which is sometimes lacking in the House of the Lord. We can put poisons upon the earth, so plentifully, but the Lord says to take care, be wise, examine your standing ground, and do nothing foolishly (See I Corinthians 11:28, Acts 17:36)

We often go through lite just doing things, without considering the result. Isn't it easy to go out on a Saturday afternoon and buy a new car? Come

Monday morning reality hits. If not then, for sure thirty days later when the first payment comes due and you think, "What have I done?"

Not too long ago, while my wife and I were outside sitting on the swing, I said, "I have an urge to spend two thousand dollars." She said, "First of all, where are you going to get that much money?" I said, "I don't know, I just have an urge to spend it." She said, "Well, what are you going to spend it on?" I said, "I don't know; we'll go find something." She said, "You know what, we just need to stay here and swing." And the entire weekend she guarded me, and did her best to keep me home. She let me go look at new trucks as long as the dealership was closed, to protect me. Haven't you faced those kinds of temptations? Be honest. Some of us wouldn't be in the mess we are in if we understood how much poison was in the pottage.

THE SPIRIT'S PRESENCE

Acts 2:1-3 says,

> *And when the day of Pentecost was fully come, they were all with one accord in one place. And suddenly there came a sound from heaven as of a rushing mighty wind, and it filled all the house where they were sitting. And there appeared unto*

them cloven tongues like as of fire,
and it sat upon each of them.

I want you to notice, the Word says, the Spirit of God sat upon each of them. God, the Holy Spirit, is already working in your life, long before the infilling. It is the Holy Spirit that persuades you to go to church on a given Sunday. You think you are there because you want to be. But God knows what will be said and He knows what you need to hear. You are there because the Holy Spirit is working, and then the utterance comes.

POISON IN THE HOUSE OF GOD

Just as there can be poison in food and poison in the work place, I believe there can be devastating poison in the House of God. I believe, in the Pentecostal movement, there is a percentage of poison. There is something wrong when a tabernacle which seats 5,000 people, but can't get more than 3,000 together for a camp meeting. I am not condemning this organization, but if you check across the board, you will find there is a spiritual famine in the land. People have lost their hunger for the Word. People have heard the same thing for so long, it no longer has any effect on them. They hear it as if they had watched a television program. In fact, they would rather stay home and watch a television program.

I believe what we have been taught about Pentecostal power is, in a lot of ways, like having poison in the pottage. Not so much by what has been said, but by what we have seen. There are many people who will shout because Sister So-n-So shouts. It may be okay for Sister So-n-So or Brother So-n-So to shout because they have been part of the upper room crowd and found something to shout about. But we get so Pentecostal that we tell folks, "Oh, just stand up and shout." The first question we need to ask ourselves is, "What do I have to shout about?" If God hasn't quickened your spirit, sit there until the quickening comes. Acts 2:4 says, "…as the Spirit gave them utterance."

We have people shouting because others are shouting. One mother spoke it so plainly. "I know my children go to the altar and fake speaking in tongues, but that's okay. I'd rather they fake it, because one day they will get it." I disagree. I'm not going to raise my children to be fakes. Right is right and wrong is wrong. I'm not going to raise my children to make a mockery of the Holy Spirit. If we teach them to fake it, that is exactly what we are doing. We are throwing rot in the pottage. I'm going to teach my children that if a spiritual tear is building in them, go ahead and cry. But until then, don't be a fake. Don't say one thing and mean another.

There are enough preachers in the congregations and pulpits across our nation who are saying one thing, but in their hearts, mean something different. If that wasn't true, we wouldn't have so many thirty, forty and fifty-member congregations. We have enough churches in America for every man, woman and child to have a place to sit. I'm not raising my children to be fakes and training them with poison in the soup. I'm going to let them know that if they touch a hot burner, it is going to burn them. I can't take that pain away, but I would like to teach them to be wise.

LIFE AND DEATH CHOICES

The decisions you make are life and death. The places you go and the choices you make are things you may live with for a lifetime. Many people are still living in tragedy because of bad choices. But you don't have to live like that forever, God can remove poison from your soup pot now. God can clean you up and help you sec. I've had people say, "Pastor, I tried getting into God, but all I did was cry. I'm a man and I'm not going to cry." I will tell you the same thing I tell them: "He washed my eyes with tears so I can plainly see."

A few years ago, I lost the ability to cry, I said, "God, if you ever give it back to me, I don't ever want to lose it. In one church, a man came up to me and said, "It's okay, Son: I see you crying in the pulpit, but you will grow up and get tough one day, I don't want to be tough. I don't want to be so "manly" that I can't give in when God speak to me.

HABITUAL PRAYER

When God speaks, the first thing He does is draw you to your knees. Until we learn how to pray, we should be saying, "Lord, I am humbled. Teach me something about prayer, praise and power." After a time, we'll be able to say, "God, I'm not going to pray because I need something, but because you said to 'pray without ceasing" (1 Thessalonians 5:17).

I like the idea of habitual prayer. Everywhere I go, I want to be praying. When people ask what I'm doing, 1 want to be able to say I'm praying. If they ask why my lips aren't moving, I'll say, "Don't worry about my lips, for man looks on the outside, but God looks on the inside. He cares about what is going on inside my heart."

Even if you are crippled in mind or body, let there be that habitual prayer. Make it a habit. One day that prayer is going to connect. It is time for Christians to come out from among the world and be a separate people. The Lord didn't say we should go out there and let everyone see how well we can pray. He said we should pray, pray, pray.

People ask how they can know if they're praying correctly. "How do I know when I am in the right vein?" they ask. You will know because the moment you get into the right vein in your prayer, you will begin praising Him. That is what good prayer will do. "Oh, Lord, I started our wanting something, but now I don't care about my needs.

I want to praise you. I want to love You, and give adoration on to You. Oh, God, it you never touch me again, you have already touched me enough. After you learn how to pray, it moves you right into true praise.

THE POWER OF TRUE PRAISE

When true praise comes, you inquire why so many have received the Holy Ghost. When true prayer comes, that awesome kind of God-praise, it is like giving candy to a baby in the eyes of the Lord we are all babies. No more poison in my soup, no more death in my pot. Devil, you enjoy the spiritual death you have bestowed upon my home, but when I get home, I'm going to kick you out. You are leaving no more death in my home.

There is a real devil and a real hell. Real prayer and real praise are the only things that will bring real power. It is time for Pentecostals to be full of power. Not just the power to shout, but the power to speak to that mountain and have it go in Jesus' name. Power! When we think of Pentecostal power, we think of shouting. When there is a shout in church, we go home and say, "Oh, my God, we had church today." I am not afraid of the shout; I told you I love it. I love going home so sore that I can't walk for three days. But power is not so much in action, as it is in knowing who you are. That is why many people shout only because Brother or Sister So-n-So shouts. They do it because they don't know who they are in Christ.

They have been sitting around for years trying to fit in. You will never fit in. If you do find someone you can fit in with, it won't be two or three weeks before they hurt your feelings. You might as well say, "There is poison in the pot." Get your eyes off man. Quit looking at the preacher and start looking at the God who is flowing through the preacher. It is God that we need. It is the cross and salvation that we seed. We need true prayer and ultimate praise and power-not a man to lead us.

Christians without the infilling of the Holy Ghost are like a gun without a bullet. Every time Barney Fife got into a situation where there was a battle to fight, he had to go find a bullet. In the twenty years I have been watching the Andy Griffith show, Barney has never, not once, shot the right thing. There are some believers I have observed since my childhood who still haven't hit their target. There is a lot of noise, attitude, and financial giving, but they are dead spiritually. That is the reality of where many people live.

GET GOING, SATAN

If there was true power in the House of God, we could speak and the devil would have to go. The devil doesn't fear you; he fears the Holy Ghost power in you. People tell me, "Pastor, I have the Holy Ghost, but 1 am still fighting the devil." That is because you have the wrong concept of the Holy Ghost. It is time we stop speaking for Him, and let Him speak for us.

It is time for us to pray, "God, I'm going to stand here and keep my mouth shut, and when you get ready for me to fight the wiles of the enemy, you will give me the words."

I told the Lord recently, "God, I know I don't have the correct English to speak things, so when the Holy Ghost comes on me and begins to flow, I speak exactly what He wants me to speak." He said, "Boy, don't worry about it. Get out of the way and I will say what needs to be said." That is why I don't apologize for what I preach. If folks don't like it, I remind them to tell God, not me. I don't let it affect me.

God is at work. Too many people have walked through the doors of our church telling me about miracles they have seen. I have to believe it. I am fired up about what God is doing. But often, we can't find complete deliverance because we are too busy shouting when we should be soaking in the teachings of the Word. We give the devil seven days a week and give God three hours out of one day and say, "I'm holy." No, you are not. You are right on the edge of destruction and you do not even realize it.

When the power is operating in your life according to the Word, you can just touch someone and the power will flow. AT&T has it right with the slogan: "Just reach out and touch someone." When the true power comes upon you, things will happen. You can stand confident, knowing that Jesus will never leave you or forsake you (Hebrews 13:5, paraphrased).

PUT FEET ON YOUR FAITH

In Mark chapter 5, we read about the woman with the issue of blood. This woman was not allowed to be with people. By law, because of her sickness, she could not be out in public. One day, she got beyond what man was saying. She may have thought, *they might kill me, cut my head off. hang me, or lock me up, but I heard Jesus was coming through town and I believe I can get to Jesus before they find me.*

When the Holy Ghost comes upon you, even though the devil tries to slay you, you can get to God in the nick of time. That woman pressed through the crowd, thinking, *If I can just touch Him, I believe with all my heart He can heal me. The key word here is "heart". I believe if I can touch the hem of His garment- -not His head, not shake His hand, not hug Him, but just touch the bem of His garment.* She stepped out in faith. She pressed through the crowd and touched the hem of His garment. Notice, not a word was spoken. She didn't ask permission; she didn't ask her neighbor. She just went. Many of us are not going to get the poison out of our lives until we get up and go.

The moment she touched Jesus' garment, He turned and asked, "Who touched my clothes?" (Mark 5:30). In modern language, the disciples said something like, "Oh Lord, come on now. We know you are the Lord. There are hundreds of people around you, with their hands touching you." Jesus just looked around to see who had touched him. In a trembling little voice, the woman said, "It is I." What did Jesus

17

say? "Daughter, twenty years from now your faith is going to make you whole." No. He said, "Thy faith hath made thee whole." She was made whole, at the moment she touched the hem of His garment.

I'm tired of religion that always promises results, in the future. I am ready for some results right now. I am ready for people to be set free now. This is a now gospel, not a later gospel. God is faithful and He is doing great works. I'm not waiting for ministry to blossom twenty years from now.

A while back I told God, "I will do anything to help this ministry grow. I'll clean toilets if I have to. I'll pick up trash in the yard, but whatever you ask me to do, let it be dynamic, something that will make a difference." About that time people started cursing me and making a mockery of me. At first it hurt my feelings, but I realized that if they cursed Christ and mocked Him, how much more are they going to curse me. So now I say, "Hallelujah, I'm doing something right because there is power in the house."

WE CHANGE, NOT GOD

Notice that God is changing our understanding and not the moving or the operation of the Spirit. The Spirit is not changing. People often say God is going to do a great work in the last day. No, He is going to do the same thing that He has always done. So, why will it seem to be greater in the last days? Because in the last days, when perilous times shall come, men are going to run and say, "I want this God." There are going to be meetings where men will stand up and say, "There is poison in your soup. There is poison in your life. You have been getting the Word on the surface, but it is time you get all the way in the Word."

When you get into the Word, it appears to have more of an anointing, a greater anointing. Either you are anointed or you're not. I've heard people say they are half saved. No you are not. You are either saved or you're not. It is not enough to say you think you are full of the Holy Ghost. Either you are full of the Holy Ghost, or you are not. He is not changing the operation of the Spirit.

THE POWER IN LISTENING

There is more power in listening to the Holy Spirit than in yelling or punching. Not one time does Jesus say, "Yell at the mountain." In Mark 11:23 it say,

> *"For verily I say unto you, That whosoever shall say unto this mountain, Be thou removed, and be thou cast into the sea; and shall not doubt in his heart, but shall believe that those things which he saith shall come to pass; he shall have whatsoever be saith."*

Most Christians are yelling and hollering without results. Not too long ago, we were in a service and most of the people were worshiping God, quietly, there was a solemn presence of the Lord. A sister was standing in the corner by herself, worshiping. I made my way over to pray with her, and just as sure as I heard Him speak, the Lord said to me, "I am going to fill her with the Holy Ghost tonight." So I gave her some instruction about receiving the Spirit and not two minutes later, the infilling of the Holy Spirit came.

I turned and there was one last family standing with all their children. God had been doing some awesome things in their lives. I looked over and it was like there was a haze between the gentleman and I. God said, "I am going to fill him with the Holy Ghost tonight." I sheepishly said, "Okay," and turned and prayed with the sister some more, thinking the haze would go away. After turning around and looking back at the man, a haze was still there. The Lord spoke again. "I said I am going to fill him with the Holy Ghost tonight." I called for that man to come and I began to speak some things into his life. I told him that I didn't know what his background was, but no matter what he did or did not know about the Holy Spirit, God was about to fill him. As the young man began to praise the Lord, he didn't hoop or holler, but God filled him with the Holy Ghost just the same. God changed his life. He later said, "Pastor, I can't sleep at night. I am so energized." I asked what he did when he couldn't sleep and he said, "I just pray."

God will put that spirit of prayer and praise on you Had I been busy shouting instead of listening, I wouldn't have heard. The Holy Spirit will not speak while you are speaking The Holy Spirit is a perfect gentleman, If in your prayer time all you are doing in rattling off your wants and sends and concerns, when does the Father have an opportunity so speak? Even my earthly father will not talk as long as I do. But, if I am silent, he will speak what is in his heart. The Holy Spirit always wants to speak. But here is the problem.

- Revelation 2:11 says, *"He that hath an ear, let him hear what the Spirit saith unto the churches; He that overcometh shall not be hurt of the second death."*
- Revelation 2:17 states, *"He that hath an ear, let him hear what the Spirit saith unto the churches; To him that overcometh will I give to eat of the hidden manna, and will give him a white stone, and in the stone a new name written, which no man knoweth saving he that receiveth [it]."*
- Revelation 2:29 says, *"He that hath an ear, let him bear what the Spirit saith unto the churches."*
- And again in Revelation 3:6: *"He that bath an ear, let him bear what the Spirit saith unto the churches."*

- Revelation 3:13 says, *"He that hath an ear, let him hear what the Spirit saith unto the churches."*
- And Revelation 3:22, *"He that bath an ear, let him hear what the Spirit saith unto the churches."*

Something intrigued me about this. Not that the scripture repeats itself, but that the Lord says, "He that hath an cat, let him hear" exactly seven tunesome time for every day of the week. You need to poll one of those verses out every day and dig into it.

THE DANGER OF A HARD HEART

In Matthew 13:15, the scriptures say,

> *"For this people's heart is waxed gross, and [their] ears are dull of hearing, and their eyes they have closed; lest at any time they should see with [their] eyes, and hear with [their) ears, and should understand with [their) heart, and should be converted, and I should heal them."*

In this passage in Matthew, Jesus quotes a prophecy directly from Isaiah 6:10. Now if I were teaching on healing, I would give the formula right here from the Word. We are the people of God, but the Word says the peoples' hearts are waxed gross.

The term "waxed gross used here can also be translated as "calloused" or "hardened."

If you have ever tried to wax an automobile, you know it is hard work. Have you ever let the wax dry and tried to wax it? So many of God's people are waxed by traditional teaching and by thinking, this is the way it is and I don't want to hear anything different. I want it the way we have always had it. Their hearts have waxed gross,

SPIRITUAL BLOCKAGE

Wax can cause other problems, too. If you have ever taken wet wax and accidentally wiped it across your windshield, you can't see through it, it blurs your vision. You would be amazed at how much blurred spiritual vision there is in the Home of the Lord.

What causes that? If any of you have children or grand children you know what it is like when a baby's bowels don't operate the way they should. It is called it constipation, and our hearts go out to that baby. There are a lot of God-given people who are spiritually blocked. If you ever see people fighting against the moving of the Spirit, or the freedom of the Spirit, they are bound up. There is spiritual blockage. The Word is coming forth in pure form, but sometimes it never gets to our hearts, because it is blocked off and goes in one ear and out the other. When there is a blockage, the biblical remedy is found in Ephesians 5:26, "That he might sanctify and cleanse it with the washing of water by the word."

When there is a blockage in your spiritual system, you can give all the money you want to, go to all the churches you want to, and shout all you want to, but until the Word can flow by the Holy Ghost, you won't get what you need.

The Holy Ghost comes in and purifies you. The sad thing is that a lot of people hear this, but don't receive it.

God wants to take us and help us understand that there is poison in the pot. Some people go to church week in and week out, and never get any spiritual freedom. They come in bound, and they leave bound. A baby's body can only take being bound for so long before that system ultimately rocks over.

The Lord sends His Word to say, "People, you are in bad condition; you are waxed over in some areas, but I want to show you true power. The power to shout is the celebration of revelation. But the power to bring results is the power of the Holy Spirit flowing through our lives into the lives of others brings results.

Back in 2 Kings, Elisha said, "Bring me meal" He took the meal, poured it in the pot, stirred it up and said, "Now give this to the people. It will be fine. In other words, the Holy Ghost affected the pot. If you allow the Holy Ghost to be your meal, He will begin to loose those spiritual bowels.

This is a hard subject, but it brings life to those who receive it. People can't receive healing or have their prayers answered because they are spiritually bound. If you have beer battling with addictions, you are stopped up in your thinking. If you are not careful, your heart will become waxed hard. You can't act like the world, persecuting and criticizing the church and then say, "Oh God, I'm Yours and I need You to work on my behalf." It is time to stop bucking the system and say, "Lord, if it takes an hour and a half for worship, then so be it. I am tired of being stopped up. Cleanse me so Your Holy Spirit can flow through me."

It is imperative that we decide, once and for all, whether we are going to live for the Lord or not. If we are, we must pray with great conviction and persuasion for God to unstop the areas in our lives that keep us from understanding the fullness of the Word. In other words, our prayers should be like King David's in Psalm 51:10, "Create in me a clean heart, O God; and renew a right spirit within me." That is our only hope of spiritual cleansing, the only sure way to get the poison out of our life's pot.

CHAPTER TWO

WHAT ARE YOU SERVING OTHERS?

Whenever the body of Christ comes together, about 90% of the people come just to be filled with the presence and love of the Lord, leaving 10% who don't know why they are there. Unfortunately, within that 10% there is always a small group who may be there to come against what God wants to do. But, I have been taught, the greater number wins.

There is so much poison in the minds and hearts of God's people. I am learning something about the Lord, though. The hollering and the shouting is awesome, but so much greater is the power in just soaking in the presence and love of the Lord. Sometimes, it pays to be quiet and listen to the Spirit of the Lord. If a congregation comes together as one, there will be enough God to put a billion to flight.

PROTECTING WHAT IS GOD'S

I have never been too weak for words. I always have something to say. And I am going to protect what God has given me. We don't have to be weak-kneed when it comes to the true gospel. Have you ever heard the old saying that there are some among us who are not right, who don't belong? There were some like that who announced they were coming after our ministry, but they would have had to get through a lot of people before they reached me. People asked if I was worried. I said, no, because I had already exposed that devil. I am going to go ahead and be bold. At the first appearance of someone like that, I am on them like a yard dog. I meet them at the front door and they are not welcomed back. Our churches are God's house, and there is no devil, no weapon, and no mouth that can tear down what God is building.

If you are right in your heart, it doesn't take a song or a message to know Gods there. But for those whose hearts are waxed gross and whose ears are dull of hearing and whose eyes are closed, there must be a change. The Word says that unless they hear, see, and unless they understand and be converted, they will not gain new, fresh enlightenment and God will not heal them.

Shallow minds spend their time looking around to see who is right and who is wrong. I could care less, because there is so much of God and so much that is right. Paul reminds us in Philippians 4:8 that if there is any good thing, we should dwell on the good!

> *Finally,   brethren,   whatsoever*
> *things are true, whatsoever thongs*
> *(are)   honest,   whatsoever   things*
> *(are) just, whatsoever things (are)*
> *pure, whatsoever things [are] lovely,*

> *whatsoever things [are] of good
> report, if (there be) any virtue, and
> if (there be) any praise, think on
> these things."*

I am going to dwell on good things. God will
bathe you with His Holy Spirit if you will allow Him
to. When the poison is gone, you get a thicker soup.
The thicker the soup, the sweeter it is. The thicker
and heavier the anointing, the less the devil can stay
and the more God bathes us.

FIND YOUR POISON

We all have some poison in the pot. If you are living and breathing then somewhere in your life there
is poison in the pot. If there was no poison in your
pot, you would be full of joy and peace. You wouldn't
have financial dilemmas. I used to think that if I
could just make more money, I wouldn't have financial needs. Do you make more money now than you
ever have, and still have money problems? Do you sit
down at the end of every month and say, "If I could
just make more money"? Making more money is not
the answer. The more we make, the more it takes. We
have to learn how to use the word "no." Whatever
heavy load you are carrying, whether it is financial or
some other kind, God can lift it.

There once was a farmer who had a nagging
wife. He started staying out in the fields longer and
longer each day because he didn't want to hear his

wife nagging him. The woman made the mistake of going out to the field one day. She no sooner got there then the Gaging began. The old farmer stopped the mule, unhooked the plow, and unharnessed the mule. The mule looked at the woman who was just nag, nag, nag, nagging, and reared back and kicked the woman, dead. The woman was laid out in the funeral parlor, as family and friends came in, the ladies looked at her, then went over to the husband and seemed so sad. As the men came in, they would go over to the husband with a different kind of expression. Now, the funeral director thought this was strange. He stood and watched until he couldn't stand it any longer. He walked over to the husband and said, "I don't understand what is going on. Can you help me? When the ladies view the body of your wife, they seem sad, and yet the men don't seem that way." The old farmer told the funeral director when the women came in, looked at her and told him how beautiful she looked. The men would come over and ask him if that old mule was for sale.

Second Kings 4:40-41 says,

> *So they poured out for the men to eat. And it came to pass, as they were eating of the pottage, that they cried out, and said, O [thou] man of God, [there is] death in the pot. And they could not eat (thereof). But he said, Then bring meal. And he cast [it] into the pot, and he*

said, pour out for the people, that they may eat. And there was no harm in the pot.

UNDERSTANDING THE SHOUT

As Pentecostals, we are accustomed to the shout. When the Holy Ghost comes upon you, if it is truly God, you can't sit there and do nothing. There is great power and great freedom in that type of worship. It is an awesome time. In the Pentecostal movement, there are those who say the really good services are the ones where there is no preaching. I differ with that because when we come together as believers, we need to learn something from the Word, something we can relate to not fifty years from now, but today. I know I have already said this, but believe me, it bears repeating. I have things in my life I need answers for today, not fifty years from now.

We talk about the shout being an awesome time in the Lord, but there is greater power when you learn how to be still. The scripture also reads that Jesus got upset in the temple. That story is there to show us that in some situations, you simply have to get bold. But for every one time that you read about Jesus getting a bit energized-like kicking the tables over in the temple you read three hundred times where He just spoke to the people. Think about the woman who was caught in the act of adultery. The mob brought her to the Lord and said," Look what she has been doing. She is sleeping with all the men in the city." Jesus did not kick her, persecute her, slice her throat, and condemn her like we do (poison in the pot). Jesus simply said as a lesson, "that is without sin among you, let him first cast a stone at her (John 8:7). Let that one who is so perfect throw the stone. And wasn't it just a few moments later that the Lord asked, "Woman, where are those thine accusers?" She told him there weren't any. What did Jesus do? He didn't shout, He didn't scream, He didn't holler. He simply spoke to her and said, "Go, and sin no more."

Remember the night on the Sea of Galilee? Peter wanted to get out of the boat and come to Jesus. Jesus didn't scream at him. He said, "Come" (Matthew 14.28-29)

Jesus said, "Whosoever shall say to the mountain, be thou removed and cast into the sea, and shall not doubt" Matthew 21:21). People say, "But Pastor, I have been speaking to that mountain for years *Yes, but you are doubting. We think, I believe God can heal me of headache, but I do not believe He can beat we of cancer. I believe if I can get in a good shouting service, oh, the Holy Ghost will do a work in me.* By now we have been in four or five hundred services and we are still sitting, wretched and miserable. In fact, there are people who don't come to church because they think it is going to be the same as it has always been: just another song, another message and another offering. They decide they don't like that music anyway, and stay home. There are people who don't go to church today because they have become complacent in their faith; things don't happen the way they think

31

it should. They claim they have tried to get in the shout, but nothing happens. That is because of a lack of understanding. The truth is, when you understand who you are in the Lord, you can look at that mountain and say, "Mountain, get out of my way."

ISSUES ON THE HOME FRONT

Many of us have been trained that unless we shout, God can't move. That is one side of dealing with poison in the pot. On the flip side, I want to deal with some issues that will help us. It is time to further expose the problems, the poison in the pot. If we are going to expose poison, it is going to hurt. Sometimes it hurts me, too. Whenever I stand in the pulpit, the words bounce off the back wall and come right back and hit my own home.

I don't know if you have noticed, but in our society today, we have major issues going on with the children. 1 agree with the law that says you can't beat your children, but on the other hand, I disagree with not being able to discipline them.

I heard a lady on television speak of a letter a little girl wrote to the Lord. "Dear God, why didn't you save the school children in Littleton, Colorado or in Santana High School recently? Sincerely, Concerned Student." God wrote back, "Dear Concerned Student, I am not allowed in schools. Sincerely, God."

Let's look at how this has unfolded in an incredibly short period of time. We are going to expose the poison in the pot. Madeline Murray O'Hare complained that she didn't want prayer in schools and the people agreed. Then someone said we had better not read the Bible in school. The Bible says thou shalt not kill, thou shalt not steal, and thou shalt love thy neighbor as yourself. We said, "That's okay, we don't need the Bible in schools, either." Dr. Benjamin Spock said we shouldn't spank our children when they misbehave, because their little personalities would be warped and we might damage their self-esteem. And we agreed and said that an expert should know what he is talking about, so we wouldn't spank them anymore. Then someone decided that teachers and principals had better not discipline our children when they misbehave. So the school administrators told the faculty members that in their school, or any school, they had better not touch a student who misbehaves, because they don't want any bad publicity and they sure don't want to be sued. We accepted their reasoning.

Someone else said we should let our daughters have abortions without having to tell their parents, we decided that was a great idea. Then some wise school board member reminded us that boys are going to be boys and they are going to do it anyway. So let's give our sons all the condoms they want so they can have all the fun they want. We won't have to tell their parents they got them at school. And we said that was another great idea. Someone said, "Let's print magazines with pictures of nude women in it and call it wholesome, down-to-earth, appreciation for the beauty of the female body. And we said we have no problem with that. Someone else took that appreciation a step further by publishing pictures of nude children, and then went a step further by making them available on the Internet. We responded that everyone is entitled to free speech.

The entertainment industry said, "Let's make TV shows and movies promoting violence, profanity and illicit sex. Let's record music that encourages rape, murder, drugs, suicide and satanic things." We called it entertainment and said it has no adverse affect and nobody takes it seriously anyway, so go ahead. It's okay with us. Some of our top elected officials said it doesn't matter what they do in private as long as they do their jobs." We agreed and said it doesn't matter what anyone-including the President of the United States-does in private, as long as we have jobs and the economy is good.

Now we are asking ourselves why our children don't have a conscience. We wonder why they don't know right from wrong. Why doesn't it bother them to kill strangers and classmates, or even themselves? Undoubtedly, if we thought about it long and hard enough, we could figure it out. I am sure that it has much to do with the biblical principle that we reap what we sow (Galatians 6:7).

KNOW YOUR CHILDREN

I know this is hard, but some people don't have any idea what is going on in their children's lives because they are so busy, being holy and righteous. Too many of us put on our nice suits on Sunday, and come to the House of the Lord saying, "All is well," not understanding that it is our child ripping antennas off cars in the parking lot. The House of God must start telling the truth in regards to undisciplined homes. But before we go out into the world and tell it, we have to tell it on the inside.

A POWERFUL LEGACY

Why do our children turn out the way they do? It starts in the home. I believe that a good, healthy family, lives on-even after the parents are dead and gone. To this day, when I go to the two hundred-acre farm my grandparents owned in Lake City, Florida, I can walk across the fields and hear the voice of my grandfather. Even though the old home place has been torn down, I can hear the morals, the standards that he lived by. He believed with all his heart that a man who doesn't work, doesn't eat. He worked to his dying day, at the age of 79. He fell dead of a heart attack on the old home place. He gave all he had. The family was astounded at what the grandparents had saved for the children to have after they were gone. At that time he was driving a 21-year-old pick-up truck. The family had said, "Boy, if we ever win the lottery, we are going to buy granddaddy a new truck. Granddaddy could have bought everyone a new truck. The point is the home is gone, granddaddy lives on. I always enjoyed granddaddy Smith convincing my mother to let me go to K-Mart with him, so I could drive. Until that time in his life, he had probably never gone 90 miles an hour in a vehicle. In fact, he would leave his teeth at home because he knew they were going to come out of his mouth along the way.

Even today, we can hear the voices of those great people who were instrumental in our lives. I am not looking forward to seeing my mother and father leave this world-I hope they are here till Jesus comes-but when the day comes that they are gone, their spirits are going to live on. They planted good values, good morals, and taught their children that if you don't work, you don't eat. They taught their children right from wrong.

The problem with our society is, we have been brain-washed into believing that since we can't spank our children, we can't teach them anything either. There is poison in the pot because of activity behind closed doors in the home.

Several years ago a frustrated mother came and cried on my wife's shoulder saying, "I don't understand. My children have gone wild. We have raised them in the church, we have taught them, and we have tried to show them the right way to go." Shortly after that she came back and cried on my wife's shoulder again. "You won't believe what my nine-year-old son found in the closet. He found pornography. I walked in and caught him sitting in the bathroom reading it." Because of the hidden sins of the father, the son found the magazines. Parents think they can hide their sin, not realizing that boys and girls know how to plunder. You would be ashamed if someone showed up and started plundering your home, Children will find what they are not supposed to find.

RIP OFF THE BAND-AID

People tell me how holy and righteous they are, but they don't understand the state they are in. If we're in the spiritual state of mind we should be in, there would be an abundance of joyful Christians. We wouldn't have to beg or plead for people to come to church. The Bible says, "For their hearts are waxed gross." For too long we have been waxed over with religion and have placed another Band-Aid on the problem. People think, Oh, they have figured me out in this church; I need to run to another church. There is too much God in that church. I can't stay there; let me come back to this one over here. 1 understand that God may move people, but He doesn't move them for the wrong reason. You can't go in the name of God and bring your sin with you. It is time for the church to expose what is wrong.

If I dealt with just one issue, it would be attitude. I have never seen children with such rotten attitudes in all my life. I thought I had a bad attitude growing up. When people ask why I think my attitude was so bad, I say, "By the measure of beatings I got." That told me something was wrong. People often tell me how holy and righteous they are at home and remind me that when they come to church, they speak in tongues. Uh-huh. That isn't how God measures holiness.

The church's bookkeeper called a family to tell them that they hadn't indicated on their check where they wanted the money to go. Those folks jumped all over her, just about cussed her out, and hung up on her. She called back and told them where she was from and they said, "Oh, God bless you and hallelujah," There are people who walk into our churches and shout all over at the front, but these same people will curse you in a heartbeat and want to know why their children are unruly,

ATTITUDE CHECK

My daughters are never tardy for school, but one day they both were, I sat them down before they left the house and said, "Now girls, I don't understand what is going on in your heads, but I have had enough of these rotten attitudes. I don't know why you suddenly want to snap at me and fight each other. You would have to want to die before you snap at me. I didn't beat them, I didn't abuse them, but they understood that while they had permission to leave with a bad attitude, when they came home, there had better be two different girls walking in the door. And they were.

The Bible says that if a man cannot rule his own home, his own household, then how can he rule or lead the House of God (1 Timothy 3:5)? I have been studying leadership recently, since we are about to do some leadership training. If you really want to know what kind of leader someone is going to be, look at their home, not how they dress. Watch how they respond when someone cuts them off on the highway. Look at how they treat the waitress. I tell people that if they are not a good tipper, they shouldn't go out to eat with me. The waitress works her hardest to give her best, we are not leaving her a quarter. Don't humiliate the church by leaving a sorry tip. Your children are watching you. If your parents were lousy tippers, break the tradition.

If we are not careful, we will teach our children bad habits and bad attitudes and put poison in the pot. There are some things I used to enjoy doing out in public that I don't do any more because I have a thirteen-year-old that insists on doing everything daddy does. I mean literally, I have had to learn to cut back on some of my fun time and help teach her the difference between the right time and the wrong time.

Instead of coming to the altar with your problems, you may need to sit there and deal with the problems in your family. Teach them how to act in the House of the Lord. Teach them that the altar is not romper room time. Church ladies shouldn't have to leave the service to care for children that do not belong to them. There is poison in the pot.

WHAT DO OUR LIVES TEACH?

Why is there such a great disregard for adults on behalf of our children? We adults are patterning our children's lives on the way we act. You can pray or sing all you want, but doesn't mean a thing except there is poison in your pot place responsibility on the House of God. For too many years the House of God has allowed this corrupt way of thinking. It has gotten to the place where there is more world in the church, than there is church in the church. I know this is tough to swallow, but this is good medicine. I have Sunday morning workers who go through unbelievable torment because of unruly children. It is a sad day in America when preschools enroll children to give them good Godly training, and we have such spoiled children that unless the workers hold a baby the entire day, that baby only cries. Many of them are from families in the House of God. I am not telling you to harm your children, but I will say this, read the Word and the Word will give you instruction. When my children need discipline, the Holy Spirit helps me discern the type of discipline they need. And the Holy Spirit should be doing the same for you.

Many of you have young people and children moving into that phase of life where they begin to develop relationships with the opposite sex. It is our job to teach them, by the Word of God, how they are to act and how they are to choose a mate for life. If we don't, boys are going to grab a girl and start abusing her like they saw daddy beat mama. They are going to say, "Well, daddy did, granddaddy did, and great-granddaddy did, so it must be right."

What you see with the natural eye may not always be good medicine for you. Elisha sent the worker to get herbs for the stew. He went out and brought back what he thought was good for food, just like you go to church because you think you will receive good teaching. But you learn more by what you see the church do, than by what you hear the church say. I learn more about people by watching them than by listening to them.

John G. Lake was at a crusade and began praying for a lady; he stopped and asked, "Didn't I pray for you last night?" And she said, "Yes sir." He said, "Then go and sit down, you are already healed, it is just your faith."

I get tired of praying for people for the same thing. We serve a God that created the universe. We serve a God who we proclaim is greater than the wiles of the enemy. We serve a God who says that when He fills us with the baptism of the Holy Spirit, we no longer have to fear life or circumstances or anything that comes against us. Yet we come in and live like sheepish believers. Either God is God or He isn't. You are either saved or you're not. When people tell me they can quote scriptures, I think big deal. I am more interested in how they live.

PARENTAL AUTHORITY

I have had people tell me they think I'm against children. No, I am not. I am tired of what the enemy is doing to the children in our society, it is time to expose the truth. The truth is, you can come in and play church all you want, but don't be surprised when you find out it is your children who are misbehaving in church. The parent should rule the home. The parent is the one in authority. I have seen parents sitting in restaurants with their little ones, trying to get their children to behave. They attempt to discipline them, the child laughs or throws something at them, and the parents laugh right along with them. Ten years from now, that child may be waving a gun, laughing and saying, "Isn't that funny?" There is poison in the pot.

Now, there are some children who are going to be rebellious no matter what their parents do. They have been raised right and yet they still rebel. We do have people that taste poison and say, "Wow, this is bad and I am going to get away from it." There are others who taste the bad and then go back and taste more, before long it doesn't taste bad anymore.

TASTE AND SEE

I am not convinced that people drink because it tastes good. They drink because their senses are numb to the real truth. Just like people come in and they sit, soak and sour in the House of God. They come in and see miracles and go home doubters. They see God healing homes. They see families where separation was inevitable, but when they gave God a chance, He healed their home. People see restored families sitting in the House of God, filled with the Holy Ghost, secure, but it doesn't affect them. In Psalm 34:8, the Word says to "taste and see." Too many taste and don't see because their hearts are waxed gross.

THE POWER OF WORDS

I never understood the power of words until I went on a camping trip with my wife and another couple about nineteen years ago. Now this friend was considerably heavier than I was, and he asked, "How do you get your wife to do what you ask?" In just making conversation, I jokingly said, "When she gets smart with me, I just slap her upside the head." Understand that I have never laid a hand on my wife, ever. Later that weekend, my friend and his wife got into an argument. He started shoving her, and pinching her on the mouth. We thought, what is going on here? Next thing we knew, he had her pinned down with his elbow in the front seat of the car, driving it into her face. My wife and I were at the picnic table wondering if he had gone crazy. All of a sudden he looked up at me and asked, "How am I doing, dude? Is this what you were talking about?" He was just as serious as life. He attacked the girl because I had told him I that I beat my wife. Never mind that I was joking. I never told another person some thing like that again, even in jest.

We often don't understand the influence we have on our children by the things that we watch on television, by the things we say, and places we go. It is not your child's fault that you overextended yourself financially and want to curse the bill collectors when they call. You know what that makes your child do? When they start receiving bills, they will start cursing and abusing, except it will be worse.

Even if you have finished raising your children, this truth applies to you. Our churches need the seasoned folks of the ministry; we need your pure faith and prayers. You can adopt some struggling mother and say," Let me help you." I'm not telling anyone to go home and harm their children. You must find a way to speak truth into their lives.

What is it like for your thirteen-year-old child to go to school terrified that someone is going to show up with a gun? My daughter came home disturbed because one of her friends heard someone say they had a gun at school. The drugs and pornography and the things that go on are scaring our children. And some of the children bringing these things to school are getting this garbage from home. You can get behind closed doors and have your ugly spats, but your children will hear them. You can hide your pretty little books, but your children are going to find them. You can get on the phone and call 1-900 while your children are listening on the other end. And, the devil is going to see to it.

STAND UP AND BE COUNTED

We need people to take a stand and start speaking the truth. We need churches willing to stand up for what is right. God is not going to come back for a corrupt church. Just because you can shout better than anyone else, doesn't make you righteous. I'm going to do my part so together we can clean up the House of God. People in our church have told me that if I preach certain messages, we are going to lose some families. I believe, for every family that leaves, God will send twenty that want to be taught. God desires for people who want to be changed, healed, delivered, and set free. We must get rid of the poison in the pot.

Some of us are in the mess we are in because we keep trying to put a Band-Aid on what is wrong. God called us to rip the Band-Aid off. I am exposing an area where the enemy has had us in the dark. It is time for the church to step into the light and be cleansed. It is time for parents to go home and cleanse their homes. It is time for people to quit bickering, complaining, and griping because the service is too long, or it's too cold or too hot, or they don't like the music. It is time to speak the truth.

DISCERNING POISON

My desire is to see a considerable difference in your faith, in my faith. I want us to be better parents. I want us to be able to identify poison in the pot. One of the greatest ways to discern whether it is poison or not, is to ask yourself, "Is this right for me?" By having to ask should let you know it isn't. It is a gray area; it is borderline.

There is a neat thing about camper trailers. They have gray water and they have a tank for sewer water. We were camping some time ago and something malfunctioned inside so I went out and pulled one of the valves thinking it was the gray water. It wasn't, it was the sewer water. Wouldn't you know that was the only time in my life that hose came off? I was a mess. My wife wouldn't even say hello to me from three miles away. She said, "Go call me and we will talk."

If even the world knows how to discern right from wrong, why should Christians sit in the House of God and continuously go home blinded? God called us to be pure, holy, and righteous.

I have a hard time dealing with people who won't come to grips with the truth. And the truth is, we are raising a society of children who don't know right from wrong. By our actions we teach them, that as long as things are going well, we don't care what they do. If a preacher says one thing out of place, the world is ready to hang him. But we let the man who leads the country live an immoral life before America's children and we shout, "Oh, what a free country. We are not free. I believe we disgust God because of a warped way of thinking.

How can we turn it around? We can say, "Lord, as a parent, I can see areas that I have been weak in, but today, I am going to make a fresh commitment." Allow your pas tor to preach the truth. If he tells you things that are not in the Word, don't receive it, don't listen to it, but as long as it is the Word, listen.

We Pentecostals point fingers at other organizations because they don't speak in tongues. You ought to stick your face in the mirror, and say, "Self, you are a miserable wreck. Look what you are raising, look at your attitude, look how you spend your money, look at your shallow worship." The hard gospel will bring a truth of deliverance so people can take a deep breath and be able to walk uprightly. Notice that Elisha didn't take something out of the soup. He added something to it. He added meal to purify, to cleanse.

It is time to start praying, "God, I want enough of Your Word in my life to consume the cancer." A member of our congregation was diagnosed with cancer that was beyond treatment. She continued to be committed in prayer and worship, God miraculously caused the good blood cells to begin to eat up the bad blood cells. Needless to say, the doctors were completely amazed. They even said that only God could cause this to happen.

Many people believe God is the one who is to resolve their bad attitudes. Really, you pass it on, from person to person to person. I am looking for people with good characteristics who can attach good things to my life. I want our churches filled with good people, so that when sinners come through the door, they can smell the sweetness of the Lord. I don't want people to come in and smell and see what they already have. You have to allow God to speak to your spirit so it can attack, corner, and slay sin. There are some things that you don't say because they hurt and attach to people, We need to be aware of what we say and how we live. We have to allow God to open our eyes.

Parents, you must stop your children from dominating your life. That is nothing more than a rebellious spirit. I want you to decide that you are going to take back control of your home before you have to stand over a casket. We are talking life and death here. There are some children who are going to be rebellious, but for the majority, we can do something about it. Children want someone who will get out front and lead. Your children want you to lead them. They need you. Undisciplined homes and undisciplined ministries produce vagabond, confused children, and poison in the pot. I believe with all my heart that we can change society, but we have to allow God to get tough in some areas, and we have to stand with Him.

I know it is very difficult to raise our children. Society hasn't helped much either. But, as we discover the poison in our homes, God is faithful to give us wisdom and strength to conquer the things that try to overtake us. Second Corinthians 4:8-9 says,

> *We are troubled on every side, yet*
> *not distressed; we are perplexed,*
> *but not in despair; Persecuted, but*

not forsaken; cast down, but not destroyed.

Ask, with persuasion, and God will help you raise your children. Ask Him to make you an example they can follow.

CHAPTER THREE

GET OFF THE FENCE

> *So they poured out for the men to eat. And it came to pass, as they were eating of the pottage, that they cried out, and said, O [thou] man of God, [there is] death in the pot. And they could not eat [thereof]. But he said, Then bring meal. And he cast [it] into the pot; and he said, pour out for the people, that they may eat. And there was no harm in the pot* (2 Kings 4:40-41).

Have you ever sat down with a meal and filled your mouth with something that didn't taste right? As I said, I always smell my food before I eat it We were with several other couples one day and were invited to share a meal with them. They asked me to pray for the food, so I looked over at my wife and asked her to pray. When she finished praying one of the ladies looked at me and asked, "Pastor did you smell your food?" I said, "You betcha, while my wife was praying."

I don't care where you are in life, whether you are a believer or a non-believer, whether you work

in the highest office of this land or live in the gut-
ter. I don't care if you have lots of friends or none at
all, there is always going to be poison in the pot. If
you live your faith long enough, eventually, it will
take hold. When you go out in the community and
begin to live your testimony, someone will always
have something to say about your faith. That usually
concerns us when we exit the church walls.

POISON WITHIN THE CHURCH

The real issue is the poison in the pot within the
House of God. "As it is written, there is none righteous, no, not one (Romans 3:10). Jesus is the only
perfect One. From that it leads down the path to us.
There is not one perfect person. Therefore if we are
not perfect, there has to be poison in the pot. If we
were to view the House of God as the pot, my desire
is to pour enough of God in so there will never be
poison in the pot.

The Word talks about the offended believer
(Proverbs 18:19). It says that it is easier to win
an entire city than to win a brother who has been
offended. Brother and sisters don't get offended out
in the world; they get offended in churches. It is my
desire to pour enough of the Word, enough of the
power of the Holy Spirit operating in each and every
life, that there would be no harm in our churches. I
want our churches to be places where hurting people
can come and find genuine answers. I want hurting
people to come, but instead of placing a Band-Aid

on what is wrong, the body of Christ will tear off the Band-Aid. The church must pour in the meal, pour in the Word, pour in the anointing to clean the wound so that people's lives will heal. It is my desire to have a church where there is no harm in the house.

TWISTED GRACE

Before we can get to that place, we first have to deal with what is wrong. There are so many who sit in the House of God pondering their wrongs, finding a reason to say, "Because of God's grace, I can live my sin. Because of God's grace, I don't pay my debts." As we read the Word we learn about God's grace, but for some reason, somehow, someway, we have betrayed the message of His grace. We have twisted the Word to say that you can keep sinning and God's grace will cover you. I'm going to tell you about God's grace. God's grace is there to keep you from sinning, not to condone your sin, and not to offer a reason to continue to sin. God's grace is there so He can touch you and pick you up, but only if you are willing to undergo a life change.

Have you ever wondered why there are so many services in the Pentecostal movement where people do not experiences the move of the Spirit? It is because there is too much poison in the pot. There are too many people who go out and live wrong. They think they can live as they wish. So many times we live out this great, holy, righteous life in public, but all along there are hidden sins; there is darkness and there is poison. We say we prayed and heard the message and were anointed and laid all over the floor, and even shouted, but we still carry our burden and our load, and conclude that God must not be real. All along we are expecting His grace to give us permission, the opportunity to live in our sin. I have had people call and say, "Pastor, 1 need a vacation. Can I take my tithe and go spend it at the beach?" People look at their children and say, "If you don't behave, I'm going to take you to the preacher." They make the preacher out to be the monster, when the parents are the monsters for not disciplining the children.

For too long we have lived in our sin; we have lived in gross darkness. We then complain when God will not come to our rescue. God will not allow you to live in sin. God will not allow you to cover up your wrongs with righteousness. You can go to church and put on a happy face, but it doesn't mean a thing when there is poison in your life. God is in the business of cleaning up the camp. We will not succeed until the coming of the Lord Jesus Christ unless we get the poison out of the camp.

No longer can we play church, no longer can we sit back and say, "Isn't God awesome?" Yes, He is awesome, but with His awesome touch comes an awesome responsibility. I have a responsibility to speak the truth and you have the responsibility to grasp and begin to live the truth. God said, "If you will expose the garbage that I show you, 1 will teach you how to build a ministry." Preaching is great, worship is awesome, but it is meaningless until we get to the core, to the root of what is wrong. We need to teach our young people that they can overcome. They already overcame. Jesus said, "I'll never leave you, I'll never forsake you, I will be with you all the way" (Hebrews 13:5, paraphrased). Understand, it doesn't matter what those on the outside say about you. It doesn't even matter what those on the inside are saying about you. What matters is that you have a meaningful relationship with the Lord. What matters is that God Almighty is working in your life. God will begin to lift you up and encourage you. God will invest His Word in your life so you can live the lite He has called you to live.

HEARING GOD'S VOICE

Some of you want to know what God sounds like. Right now He sounds like Donald R. Vining. If God gives it to me and I teach it, then God ordained me to speak into your life. Don't be distracted. It is so easy to be distracted from what God wants to say, I hope you open your mind and your heart and begin to understand, because God is not going to be satisfied until the poison is gone.

GET OFF THE FENCE

In Revelation 3:14-17, the scripture says,

> *And unto the angel of the church of*
> *the Laodiceans write; These things*

saith the Amen, the faithful and true witness, the beginning of the creation of God; 1 know thy works, that thou art neither cold nor hot: I would thou wert cold or hot. So then because thou art lukewarm, and neither cold nor hot, I will spew thee out of my mouth. Because thou sayest, I am rich, and increased with goods, and have need of nothing, and knowest not that thou art wretched, and miserable, and poor, and blind, and naked:

What God is basically saying here is, "I want to know what side of the fence you are on." Either you have a mind to make it or you don't. Either you are going to be an alcoholic the rest of your life, or you are not. Either you are going to be bound by the things of the world, or you are not.

God is ready to know where His people stand. God decided a long time ago that His people needed a Savior so He sent His Son. He could have sent a rock, but I believe Jesus said, "I'll go for you, Father. I'll go on behalf of those people, but Lord let the Holy Spirit go before me." Jesus made a commitment to come to give His life so we could have life. We get excited when mama and daddy give us a twenty-dollar bill, but think about what Jesus bore for us. Think about how they cursed Him, spit on Him, kicked Him, made Him carry His own cross, hung Him on a dunghill, and made a mockery out of Him. All so that you and I can experience life. Thank God for a risen Savior. Thank God for the commitment of the Father, the Son, and the Holy Spirit.

Where does your commitment need to change? He said, "I wish you were hot or cold, but then because thou art lukewarm, and neither cold nor hot, I will spew thee out of My mouth." God is telling us, "You think you are in one condition, but you are blinded. Your hearts are waxed gross. You think because you can go to church, all is well. You think because you gave your offering, all is well. Listen, the devil can walk an aisle and give money. You think because you are a part of worship, all is well? The devil was the chief musician. God said, He wishes we were hot or cold-He longs to know where we stand. Because we won't make a commitment, He will spew us out of His mouth. For those who have a difficult time understanding this, it simply means we make Him sick. We make God sick when we say one thing and live another. Some will say, "Well, preacher, I have a calling on my life. So what. I do too, but I would rather be able to see that calling than have someone tell me. If there is a song in my heart, I want to be able to sing that song so that someone can see that there is a God in my life, instead of me having to rum around and say, "Look at me."

TRIED BY FIRE

Revelation 3:18 says,

> *I counsel thee to buy of me gold tried in the fire, that thou mayest be rich; and white raiment, that thou mayest be clothed, and [that] the shame of thy nakedness do not appear; and anoint thine eyes with eyesalve, that thou mayest see.*

The Lord is telling us He wants to get our attention. This is life or death, success or failure, heaven or hell, joy or depression. I believe the Lord is saying to us, "I counsel with you; I want you to understand. I am asking you to give me a chance in your life. I am asking you to recognize the poison, throw it out, and buy of Me good things. Buy of Me, My Word that has been tried by fire." Some of us are trying to find an avenue or a way we can make it in this life. Try the Word. The Word has stood the test of time, throughout the course of history. If the Word stands, then why do we have to go out and recreate the wheel? Why don't we just say, "Lord I am going to buy into the Word. Lord, I give You my attention. I will no longer live in sin and call grace my avenue to live in sin. You would be amazed at those who are guilty of living wrong, all in the name of God.

God is ready for the camp to be cleansed. It is going to take the entire group of men and women of God, collectively, unified in the Spirit of God, allowing God to counsel them and show them their wrongs. It isn't a bad thing to find out that there is something wrong in your life. It is a bad thing to do nothing about it. It is okay to say, "Lord. Here I am, expose me, show me where I am wrong, so that I can be made right. There are so many sanctimonious people who come into the church and say, "Well, I am all that." Naaman was all that too, but he was a leper. The Lord is saying to his people, "There is some sin, some darkness, and there are some areas I need to deal with. Let me counsel you and show you what is wrong by My Word which has been tried by fire."

Where does gold get its strength? In the fire, where the impurities are burned away. God wants us to buy from Him gold, tried by fire, so He can point out the wrongs in us and cleanse us from them. Do you know what is wrong with the church? There are too many preachers sitting around looking for sin in their brothers, when all the time the Lord is saying, "I counsel thee that you would buy of Me gold that has been tried by fire, so that your darkness, your sin would not be found out. Allow Me to deal with the poison."

We think God can't bless us until we expose the wrongs of others. Why are we so busy trying to expose everyone else's wrong? He wants to show us how to be clothed with holiness and righteousness. All we have to do is let Him teach us. Let Him show the way and help us. If we let Him, He will speak like no man can speak.

God does not deal with you because He is mad at you. The Word says in Nahum 1:3, "God is slow to anger and great in power." God is not an angry God; He just doesn't like what the devil has done in our lives. He knows that greater is the Holy Ghost in us than the devil who is against us. That is why I beg you to fill yourself with the Holy Ghost and fire, because as long as the Holy Ghost is there, there is no devil that can come against you and conquer you. Thank God for the truth. The truth is we sometimes walk around in gross darkness, thinking, we have it all together, but we don't. When is the last time you went out and told someone about the miracle in your life? I tell someone just about every day how I was full of leukemia and God healed my body. There is power in my life because God took out the poison in my blood and replaced it with His blood. There was a time in my marriage when things were not good and I didn't know whether we would make it or not, God spoke to my heart, "If you will let Me counsel you, I will show you the way. I'll show you how you can make it. All you have to do is love ach other the way My Son loved the church and that means being willing to give your life for each other. And when you are willing to give your life for each other, you will quit treating each other like garbage."

His grace heals the sinner, and His mercy heals the saint. It is time to quit living in gross darkness. People say they want their home to be a happy place, but they won't do anything to make that happen. You can rot in your sadness. But, if you are ready for your home to be different, allow God to change your life and your attitude. You are not all that you think you are anyway. God finally got that through to me. He humbled me and helped me understand that even the best friend in the world can turn his back on you, even a great marriage can go through struggles, finances can turn upside down and the church can kick you in the head. But the Lord said, "I am a friend that sticketh closer than a brother. I will never leave you, I'll never forsake you" (Proverbs 18:24). Why is that, Lord? I believe He would say it is because He made a commitment, an investment in us, and predestined us before the foundation of the world. No one can take us out of His hands. Get the poison out of the pot, out of the soup of your life. Allow God to take out what is wrong and replace it with what is right.

WHAT IS IN YOUR CAULDRON?

The world is full of cauldrons. My father had a sugar cane mill. He would raise sugar cane and at a certain time of year, he cut the cane. He would set up his grinding mill and tie a fifty-foot cypress log to it. Instead of having a mule turn the mill, he used a tractor. He would hook the tractor to the pole and make us kids drive round and round. That was the easy part. The person standing there feeding the mill had the hard part. If you didn't duck just in time that pole would knock you out. I am convinced my father didn't need me to work as much as he was trying to knock some sense into my life. Every now and then we would slip the tractor into a higher gear and really get that thing going.

After we ground enough cane, we got a pot filled with filthy, nasty cane juice. It isn't worth taking a cup full and drinking. It is like drinking sweet mud. But in the early morning my father would begin the cooking by building a fire under the pot of cane juice. What is God doing? He is building a fire under your pot. He is trying to say that your cauldron is full of worldliness; your cauldron has been full of religious acts. Your worship has been tainted. He said he was building a fire with His Word; not to hurt us, but to help us.

My father cooked that cane juice for hours upon hours upon hours. As that juice began to cook, when it got to a certain temperature, all the garbage would boil to the top. They call that candy. It was the nastiest candy I ever saw. The workers would use rags to skim off everything that was coming to

The top. They spent hours and hours getting the garbage out. "Daddy what do you want me to do?" I'd ask. And he would say, "Skim. Wash that rag out and skim some more. Put more wood on the fire. Something is about to happen." When we get to the place in our spiritual lives where God is about to break through, many of us say, "That is enough." If the workers had quit in the middle of cooking the cane juice, we never would have had syrup. But the

61

more they skimmed, and the hotter the fire got, the more garbage floated to the top. I don't remember whether we started with fifty or a hundred gallons of juice, but we ended up with about eight or nine gallons of pure, sweet syrup. At the end, when it changed from filth to syrup, it only took minutes. I watched a young man standing at the altar one night. I didn't know if he had ever received the bap-

tism of the Holy Spirit and I asked him if he had ever spoken in tongues. He said, "No sit, all I know is that it just happens." In just minutes, by allowing the heart to be enlightened, God came in and the precious gift of the Holy Ghost came, and that boy said, "My life has never been the same; it will never be the same." Why is God suddenly baptizing and filling people with the Holy Ghost? Because He is beginning to turn up the flame. As He turns up the flame, the Holy Ghost will teach us. The Holy Ghost will get us out of our mind's eye and put us in the spirit eye. When the Holy Ghost wakes us up at 2 o'clock in the morning, instead of saying, "Lord, what is it You want now?" The Holy Ghost will say, "Boy, get up and walk, get up and write. I want to show you something that you have never seen before."

I am sure some of you are thinking, Amen to what you are saying, but I am not buying it. That is where the poison is. But when you get tapped in, and tuned in, you come to a place where you don't care what the Lord wants; you are just glad that He counts you worthy for Him to want some thing from you. You ought to count it an honor that Jesus loves you too much to leave you the way you are. You should be shouting and praising God because He loves you and wants to help you change and make you what He designed you to be. That is what He is doing in your life.

THE POISON OF LAZINESS

Laziness is killing the body of Christ. Laziness is killing good homes. Laziness is poison. There are people I have prayed for to whom I have finally said, "Until you get rid of your laziness, it does neither one of us any good for me to continually pray for the same thing over and over again." Those very people have not been back to ask me to pray for them. You know why? They don't want to hear the truth. They want the preacher to make them feel better about their wrong. "Oh, but Pastor," they wail, "you don't understand. God told me I don't have to work." The Word says that a man that doesn't work, doesn't eat (2 Thessalonians 3:10), God does not contradict Himself.

My Bible tells me that confusion and fear is not of God, but of the devil (1 Corinthians 14:33). When you come to me with a confusing message, I will not receive it. I am not going to be confused with your warped way of thinking. Don't expect the church to feed you because you are too lazy to work. Our ministry has given out hundreds of dollars to those in need, but often, they never return. People faithfully ring the phones off the hook and faithfully attend, but the moment we give them a dollar, we never see them again. I have helped raise money for people and next thing I hear is how everyone is against them. If the church was so against them, why and the church give them money? This is feeding and baiting people's laziness. I have learned this the hard way, because God knows I am a giver. I have given until the book-keeper has said, "Pastor, how do you think we are going to pay the bills if you keep doing this?" I have been more than faithful to people who are too sorry to help themselves. It is time for the poison to be exposed and come out of the por I am tired of helping people live their life when they are too lazy to live it themselves. God said, "Go to work." I know this is some hard teaching. If Jesus showed up at your house today, He would probably do what He did in the temple. He would go and kick over the tables in your living room. He won't accept your excuses; He won't put up with them. He gave His life so you wouldn't have poison in your life.

I am not trying to hurt anyone. I am trying to expose what the devil has done in our lives. Many are so burdened down by what their children have said about them. Quit listening to that garbage. You are a good mom. You are a good dad. You are a good Christian. Quit letting people put condemnation on you. Romans 8:1 says,

> *There is therefore now no condem-*
> *nation to them which are in Christ*

*Jesus, who walk not after the flesh,
but after the Spirit.*

Laziness is a poison if ever there was one in the pot.

We have talked about the power in the shout and the power in listening to the Spirit. We have found it to be true. There is much power in listening. We have talked about the poison of undisciplined homes. Now we are talking about the laziness that kills good people. We must take a stand and encourage people to stand on their own two tees. I have enough poison to deal with on my own without taking on yours. Get rid of your laziness in the physical and spiritual arena. Don't say that you are a Christian, and then live a lukewarm life. Jesus said, "For that reason I will spew you out of my mouth" (Revelation 3:16). I am upset with the devil, because of what some people have made the church out to be. Our thinking is warped.

My place is to expose the enemy in your life, but if you don't want the enemy exposed in your life, then you are not going to be happy. I deliver the truth. I bring men together and teach them how to stand on their own two feet. I teach people how to get to the root of the problem. God said He was tired of Luke warmness. He is ready for a people who will stand. He is ready for a people who will get full of the Holy Ghost. He is ready for a people who will stop griping and grumbling and complaining. He is ready for a people who will say, "Lord, whatever it takes to clean up my life, clean it." That is what God is looking for.

Laziness is killing good marriages. I told our congregation not to bring me any more family members who are living in sin and ask me to marry them. I am not going to marry them. Until couples have proven that God has made a definite change in their lives, no more weddings for me. If I marry a couple like that, all I am doing is giving them license and permission to live in their sinful ways. God has said He's had enough of the sin, already. He wants people to get married for the right reasons. People tell me I don't understand their loneliness. Jesus said that He was a husband to the widow lady. What more kind companion could you have than to give God the chance to be your husband? Men, what greater opportunity than to have Jesus hook up with you and teach you that your loneliness is not based on a relationship, your loneliness is related to you not having the right relationship with Jesus.

There are men who get married thinking, I said I do and now she is going to do everything I tell her. That is a sick way to live. We are going to clean up the body of Christ. Many of you have treated your spouses so badly in the name of God that they are numb, but you are still sitting there saying, "It's their fault." You say you provided a good living. Big deal. The devil can provide a good living. It is the love and passion that Jesus spoke of when He said He wanted men to love their wives the way Christ loves the church. That means you love them. When one hurts, you all hurt. When she hurts, you feel her hurt. Instead of fanning the flame, you try to take the flame away. We must understand that we are here to love and help.

ACTIONS TELL THEIR OWN STORY

The way you treat your family displays the level of God in your life. When you curse them, harm them, humiliate them, and misuse them, you can stand up and give all you want and shout all you want your actions speak more loudly than your words. Laziness is killing good families. What is wrong with looking at your child or your spouse and saying, "I love you?"

Laziness is killing relationships and friendships, too. We all have people in our lives who are only our friends when they need something. You know the type. I had a fellow call and say, "Hey, Brother Don how are you doing? The Lord has laid you on my heart. I thought, Wow we haven't heard from them for a long time. We talked a while about our families and how everyone was doing. Before long he said, "Oh by the way, we are having a meeting at our home Friday night and we would like for you to come." You know what I said? "You are a sorry dog." My wife gave me that look. All they did was bait me to go to an Amway meeting. That is not a true friend. A true friend will stick by my side when I am at my lowest moment. Sorry, lazy friendships are killing people spiritually. We need to expose the poison in the pot. When you get the poison out of the pot, God will begin to bless on your behalf. I am ready for God to go before me.

It's not an easy thing to allow the Lord to expose the impurities in our lives. But, when we allow it, God will not only expose situations, He will make a way of escape. By allowing the Lord to clean out the poison, not only will others see God in you, but you will feel like a brand new person. Take some time and allow the Lord to bring you to a higher level of living. Say to this poison, "In the name of Jesus, by the blood of Jesus, get out, you are not staying, deliverance is mine."

CHAPTER FOUR

CLEANING UP YOUR CAULDRON

When we expose poison in the pot, we can begin to live the true life. This life is to be a life of happiness, joy, and peace. Especially when trials and tribulations come, we should have a degree of peace and joy. As the church, I think sometimes we fall short in teaching that to the whole body. Our churches should reach out to all ages, beginning with the infants and going all the way through the golden years of life. We should desire churches that minister to the total person, the total need.

I don't believe we have to lose one person to the enemy's camp. To keep that from happening, we must build ministries that will speak the truth, the whole truth and nothing but the truth. We also have to understand that the truth hurts. In our church, the Lord seems to have established a pattern. At least two times every year, we go into a sermon series that I call "cut and dry." It is the kind of gospel you receive or reject; there is no in between.

We can talk about faith, shouting, glory, and giving. Those are fun things. But, there are times when the Lord uses the ministering of His Word to expose dark places, dark issues. Places that no one talks about. Places that are embarrassing for you to live in, much less have someone talk about.

I don't think I can say this enough: God loves you too much to leave you the way you are. In fact, I believe God knows your heart better than you do. Just when I think I have myself figured out, boy, does He show me a new chapter. He never seems to reveal things that I like about myself. He presents things I don't like. And if I don't like them, then He must not like them.

GETTING THE STINK OUT

Through the teaching and the admonition of the Word, He wants to teach us to get the garbage out. You can't take the garbage out if it has not been exposed. Let me put it this way: when you take the less desirable parts of a chicken, wrap them in a nice clean garbage bag and set them out in the garage, on about the second day, as the Word would say, "By now it stinketh." By now we should be finding some things in our lives that stink. That isn't a bad thing. It is only bad if we keep on stinking.

God will expose only as much as you can handle. Once you can handle what He wants to expose and the necessary change, He will take you to another place-another level. In other words, He will pour a little more out on you. Let's get rid of that myth that says we are saved, sanctified and filled with the Holy Ghost-and that's all there is to it. I believe in those three things, but I also believe that the seed of sanctification is planted at salvation. We will spend a lifetime being sanctified. I do not believe that all three happen at the same time and not do anything else. Too many Christians say, "Praise God, I am sanctified. I don't need to go to church anymore. Even though I've never had any teaching, I don't need any now." I've been guilty of teaching that in the past, but now I am finding that sanctification is a process. I am not real sure if I am a good husband right now, but I know I am better than I was twenty years ago, or my wife wouldn't still be here. I'm not always sure if I'm a good Christian, but I am better than I was. I'm not sure if I am a very desirable person to be around, but I'm sure of one thing; I'm better than I was thirty-eight years ago.

Through the process of sanctification, the Lord teaches us that it is better to give love than to receive love. In exposing the darker places, the poison in the pot, we have to allow the Lord to talk about issues we have neglected to deal with for a long time. By exposing these areas, God is planting another part of the seed of sanctification. Now, it is our responsibility to live it out.

When you find something wrong in your marriage, if you keep it there, things will always be wrong. When you expose what is wrong, things get better and the relationship gets sweeter with time. I believe the longer I serve the Lord, the sweeter He gets. The more we, as Christians, come together and the more we get to know each other in Christ, the sweeter the fellowship. I'm not necessarily talking about knowing the details of each other's personal lives. If you knew my personal life, you wouldn't like me (I don't mind if there are twelve pairs of shoes in the living room, and it doesn't bother me to wear smelly socks at the table). But the more we get to know each other spiritually, the sweeter our relationship gets. The sweeter the relationship-in other words, the more poison we deal with and get out of our lives the sweeter the House of the Lord.

KNOWING WHAT TO PUT IN

I want to focus on how Elisha dealt with the problem of the poison in the pot. If it worked for him, then I am sure it will be good enough for us.

Second Kings 4:41 reads,

> *But he said, Then bring meal. And he cast [it] into the pot; and he said, pour out for the people, that they may eat. And there was no harm in the pot.*

Sometimes we throw good food out because we don't know what to make with it. Sometimes, we throw good relationships away because the other person won't live the way we think they should. Maybe we are wrong, thinking they should live a certain way. Sometimes we raise wayward children because we are preoccupied with pointing out their faults and forget the only life-models they have are their parents. We need to lock the back door and figure out what we need to insert to make it right. Elisha basically said, "No problem, bring some meal. Pour meal in the pot, stir it up, and feed the people." The Bible says there was no more death in the pot. In other words, when we identify a problem in our lives, we must go the resource manual, the Bible, and find the antidote to bring us deliverance in that area.

We have talked about power: the power to shout versus the power to listen. It is an awesome thing in the Pentecostal movement to shout. People come from other denominations just to experience the energy I love a good shout, but on the flip side, I gain amazing strength from standing still, listening, and hearing. It is one thing to shout what you think you heard, but it is another thing to march to what you know you heard. As I said before, there are people that design a service in their minds and classify this a good service: there was no preaching and we shouted.

God was in our house. If it was all shouting and no teaching, where would we be if tragedy came? We must have the teaching and the shouting.

You can't live from shouting, but you can live from listening. The Spirit of God will never mislead you. You can say, "God, I won't like what you reveal, but go ahead, show it to me, because it will make me better. It will help me."

SPIRITUAL DRUNKENNES

Another poison I want to talk about is drunkenness.

Not necessarily as a result of alcohol, because we all know the repercussions of that. I could share story after story of people who have either lost their lives or whose liver is eaten up by it. I have taken part in many funeral services. Where alcohol had literally destroyed the person, the flesh. We don't need to talk about what alcohol will do, but let's examine at another kind of drunkenness that can destroy.

The Biblical Illustrator says that the vines Elisha's workers threw into the pot had three gourds: pleasure, drunkenness and misery-all three being poison. Drunkenness is not always about what it does to you, as an individual, but what it does to the people and property around you." Drunkenness takes away everything that is sacred in the family, it takes everything that is holy in religion, everything that is infinite in the soul, and tramples it into the mire." Drunkenness takes everything that is moral and slams it into the ground. Drunken living means I receive a paycheck on Friday and have nothing left on Monday morning. It means I don't even have enough money to get to work. Drunken living means spending your life on alcohol, but it can apply to other things, too. It can mean that you spend your life spending money. You make a good living, but you never have anything to show for it. I told my wife that I have worked since I was twelve years old and feel I have nothing to show for my labor. We go out and work for a lifetime, but at the end of the road we have nothing to show for it. I told my wife we were going to start being good stewards. Many people live their lives not knowing where or why they spend their money, they spent it and live another year with no benefit. Drunkenness is undisciplined living. It is nothing more than poison in the pot. It will kill you.

There are not too many God-fearing, good-natured, great moral women who desire to be married to a man who lives like a bum his entire life, lest she be a bum also. But there are some men like that out there. You need to take a good look at your surroundings. You need to take a look at what you call a friend. Drunkenness with friendship will kill a good marriage. In other words, a man or woman who will live a slothful life will never make a good partner in a relationship.

We can go through the rest of our lives spending money like a drunkard and treating people like a drunk does. But let me tell you what will happen. If you treat your family like a drunk treats his family, in the end you are going to get what a drunk gets: nothing but death.

A lady came to me a few years ago and simply said, "I don't know what is happening. My family is slipping away and my husband is hanging out at the bar with all the singles." This lady's husband would go out week after week and drink, drink, drink and then come home and get sick as a dog. He would barely make it to the kitchen sink before he lost everything that he had spent the week's money on. No wonder they couldn't clothe the children. This is what poison does to the pot. His wife kept telling him, "You are going to keep on until you throw your guts up. You are going to keep on until you destroy yourself."

One day she cleaned a chicken and left the innards in the sink. He came home that night at two o'clock in the morning, drunk. He made it to the sink, did his number and went to bed. When he got up the next morning, he said, "Baby, I have been delivered. I will never drink again." She asked, "Why is that?" He said, "You have been telling me that I was going to throw my guts up, and I did that last night. It took all I could do to get them back down." That is a funny little story, but too many Christians are destroying their lives with a drunken way of living. They don't treat their families properly. They don't treat their children right. They don't treat the House of God right. They don't treat God right. They don't spend their money the way they should.

When was the last time you asked, "Lord, is this right for me?"

GETTING THE POISON OUT

My job is to expose the poison in the pot. I want to talk to you about the next step, how to clean up your act. How do you change the pace of this poison that is running ram pant in your life? The Bible said that when Elisha came to Gilgal, there was a famine in the land. He sent servants out to gather herbs, and they gathered all they could find. It all looked good. Sin looks good. That cigarette looks good, that alcohol looks good, that pretty thing across the fence looks good, that handsome thing walking down the road looks fine. The herbs looked good. The Bible said that they didn't just gather a few, but they gathered a lap full. They loaded up. The only thing I can liken that to is the first pot of chili my wife and I ever made. Neither one of us knew any better, so we put the whole pack of hot chili powder in the pot. It was so hot we couldn't eat it, when we threw it in the backyard, we burned out the roots of every tree in the yard.

The servants threw in the herbs, mixed them up, and said it was ready to serve to the people. Elisha served the people, but someone had tasted enough of God to know that something was wrong.

The Spirit of discernment is life and death in this day and time. Some of us have lived with sin and poison for so long, we have lost our discernment. We know it looks good, but we doubt if it is good or not. We know it tastes decent, but we don't know if it is healthy for us. That long-ago day in Gilgal, someone in the crowd said, "Oh, man of God, there is death in the pot." Isn't it amazing they were unaware of the death in the pot until they had a taste! When your heart is right with the Lord, the moment you taste, see, touch, or feel something that is not Godly, something inside you will say, "That is wrong."

I am to the point where I ignore the fact that people make fun of me smelling my food. It's okay, because I am not going to eat something that is bad.

I don't love anyone enough to die from their cooking. If you ever saw what goes on behind closed doors in some restaurants, you would start sniffing your food, too. The sons of the prophets had enough of God in them to know that something was wrong and they told the man of God there was a real problem. What do we do when we have realized that we lived right and did all the right things, spent our money on what we thought was right, gave in the offering, and did everything we knew was right to do and find out that were we spent our money was poison? There was death in the pot. What do we do? Too many of us run out and start blaming God. What did Elisha do? He told the men to get some meal.

KEEP AADDING

Most of us live such shallow faith that once we have given; we have to give again. Some of you think I have fallen off my rocker. Well, I have already given and it hasn't done any blessed good. Elisha didn't throw the pot out the back window, did he? He told the men to bring him some meal. He decided to take the soup and add to it, and keep adding until he got it right. That same principle applies to how you live life. You keep adding until you get it right. You get up in the morning and try another day of marriage until you get it right. You get up in the morning, knowing that you messed up as a parent yesterday, but today, you are going to try this thing until you get it right. You decide to keep serving God until you get it in your spirit. You praise Him until you feel the presence of the Lord.

A lot of us are one-chance people. We give God one chance, and that is it. I want you to notice that Elisha poured meal in the pot, stirred it and then said, "Pour out for the people, that they may eat." And it says there was no more harm in the pot. He didn't throw the whole mess away. When your marriage is not right, don't throw your spouse away. When you're tired of your money not doing what you think it should, don't quit working. When the Pastor doesn't respond the way you think he should, don't vote him out just yet. When the roof is leaking in your home, don't burn the house down. That is what they make those big buckets of tar for: to repair the damage. Just because someone may not be acting right, we should not reject them.

The meal was symbolic of the anointing and the Word of Almighty God. When we find there is poison, we should use Elisha's example and pour some more God into the situation through His Word. Pour some love in the pot. I used to want my wife to respond to me when I made demands. I have learned if I love her the way I want her to love me, I don't have to place demands; she just loves me all day long.

The goal of exposing the poison, the death in your life, is not for you to turn against your religion, or your family, or your boss. The goal, very simply, is to encourage you to get under some good Godanointed teaching and remain there until you get it. Get this truth into your spirit. Decide that you're going to keep trying this thing until you become a good husband or wife. Decide you are going to keep loving your children until you can love them with all your heart. Decide you will keep blessing the House of God until it becomes one blessed house.

It is time to say, "I know my house is ugly, and the ceiling leaks, but I thank God for what I have." When you begin to thank Him for what you do have and begin to treat your family like royalty, they will begin to treat you that way, too. Why? Because you have exposed the poison.

This is one of the ways the enemy confuses good, God fearing people. Have you ever been moved to give a seed faith offering and nothing happens? Have you ever given money in church and then had a flat tire when you got out to the parking lot? Then the devil came right up and said, "Idiot, you should have kept your money. Now the preacher is going to ride a dolphin at Sea World with your money." And we listen to this garbage.

Don't destroy your home just because there is something wrong. Get enough of God and enough of the Word in your life that righteousness begins to drive out what is wrong. Do you want a home that is blessed financially? Do something really dumb. Give like you have never given before. I mean, give until it hurts. Watch if you are not the one still standing in the end. Do you want your marriage healed? If she spit in your face, keep loving her, keep telling her how great she is, and eventually she will get the message and change her actions. If you want God to bless you with a new home, start taking care of the one you have now.

I give the Lord permission to take areas where He has exposed darkness, poison, and death in my life and allow Him to deal with those issues. And the way He is going to deal with them is for me to get in the Bible and hear thus saith the Lord. If He tells me to go dip in the muddy water seven times, then get out of my way. I am headed for the water. If He tells me to give another hundred dollars, then get out of my way. The antidote for death is to put more of God in. When Elisha found the spring of Jericho unsuitable to drink, he did not strive to draw out the evil; he put salt in it to counteract it (2 Kings 2:20-21). When Moses found the waters of Mirr bitter, he put in the tree to sweeten them (Exodus 15:25). Every time you find something negative, put more of God in its place. About six years ago a young lady told me that serving God was really tough and if it didn't get any better, she was going back to the world. Don't you dare let the devil sell you that bill of goods. When things are upside down, when there is poison, run to God like you never have before. You give and you praise Him and surround yourself with good, Godly people. I don't mean people who have all the answers, but people who will stand and under-gird you and help you walk through it. Don't you dare run out on God. Don't you throw your soup bowl out the back door. Stand, and say, "God fill me with meal, with your anointing, with your Word." If it worked for Elisha, it will work for you.

CHAPTER FIVE

THE CLEANSING POWER OF WISDOM

While the scripture is plain in pointing out areas in our lives, our homes, and our churches that may be poisoned, God will never show us what is wrong without giving us a way to correct the wrong.

Isaiah 1:18 says,

> *Come now, and let us reason together, saith the LORD: though your sins be as scarlet, they shall be as white as snow, though they be red like crimson, they shall he as wool.*

Isaiah's first message of condemnation is aimed at his own countrymen in Judah. Judah is riddled with moral and spiritual disease, the people are neglecting God as they bow to ritualism and selfishness. But Yahweh graciously invites them to repent and return to Him because this is their only hope of avoiding judgment" (Biblical Illustrator).

Wisdom is one of the key elements God uses to deal with poison. God uses wisdom to call us together to reason. When I speak of the church throughout this chapter, I am not just referring to a denomination. All of God's children make up the church.

There are some elements that are vitally important if we are going to be what God intends us to be. I want to talk about the word "wisdom." I have found in my life that just a touch of wisdom goes a long way. Wisdom has nothing to do with education, who you know or what side of the track you came from.

Wisdom is a vital survival tool for those in Christian leadership. If we expect people to follow us, and come to be a part of our walk with the Lord, somewhere along the line we are going to have to plug in that one word. Wouldn't you like to have more wisdom?

Colossians 4:1-6 says,

> *Masters, give unto [your] servants that which is just and equal; knowing that ye also have a Master in heaven. Continue in prayer, and watch in the same with thanksgiving, Withal praying also for us, that God would open unto us a door of utterance, to speak the mystery of Christ, for which I am also in bonds: That I may make it manifest, as I ought to speak. Walk in wisdom toward them that are with out, redeeming the time. Let your speech (be) always with grace, sea-*

*soned with salt, that ye may know
how ye ought to answer every man.*

If I could added word to verse six, it would be the word "actions." Lo, let my actions be actions of wisdom. Verse five says, "Walk in wisdom toward them." We must understand that the church is not for us, but for those who are seeking, hurting, and without Christ. Walk in wisdom toward those who need a place of healing. In Colossians 4:5, the Bible also talks about the wise and winsome walk. We must redeem the time and seek out those who are without, those who haven't found what we have in the Lord.

If there is anything the body of Christ needs, it is wisdom. If there is anything that ministry lacks, it is wisdom. There are a number of great people out there, but very few with good, Godly wisdom. Christ's mission was to outsiders and so was His commission to the disciples. Christ did not come for those who were saved. He came for those who were lost. He did not come for those who were fine; He came for those with hurts.

THE CHURCH'S TRUE FOCUS

The church's focus should not be what kind of program we can build to soothe our wants, but what kind of program we can build that will touch the hearts of those that come and help us deal with the poison in the pot. You have one shot with visitors. You either succeed or not. There is an amazing influx of visitors to our churches who come to look, to seek. If we were to use a percentage, we would say that about seven or eight percent stay. The other ninety plus percent say they will be back, but never see them again, Is it possible that the ministry is not using the right kind of wisdom to keep these folks? I know the argument that says we are not going to keep everyone, and it is true. But we should keep more than seven percent.

Everyone who comes into our churches not only enters into a relationship with Christ and the church; they also have a relationship with the world. Therefore the church must use much Godly wisdom to keep them. Matthew 5:16 teaches us to,

> *"Let your light so shine before men,*
> *that they may see your good works,*
> *and glorify your Father which is in*
> *heaven."*

Notice it doesn't say they should hear about your good works, but they should see your good works.

Outsiders watch Christians closely and Christ intended that they should. Outsiders watch those who say they are Godly. As though with a magnifying glass, they are watching you, peeking through the cracks, watching you in the community. They are listening to see if you are really all you say you are. The Christian is the only Bible the great majority of people ever read. If that is true, we ought to live so that we require no commentary to explain us. We should have a straightforward way with our ministry methods. Wisdom says we should have such a way with our approach to guests that when they leave, they don't have to get out a commentary to explain what they experienced. If I was a visitor and knew nothing of the Pentecostal movement, there would be more times than not, when I would go home and say, "Wow!"

We must find Godly wisdom. We are the door-keepers to the way of life-not to block the way, but to let others in. We are the ones that open the door to heaven's way.

We are the ones who have the message. We are the ones who are saying to a lost and hurting community, "Come, we have the answer for the poison in your life."

When they get here, we must not let our method block them from seeing the real Christ.

The Biblical Illustrator puts it this way: "Walk wisely, so as not to give lie to our professions." We tell the unconverted that Christianity will make them cheerful under trials, but do we fret when we are under trials? We tell them that this is a life of joy and happiness, but how do we act when things go wrong in our own lives?

We talk about patience. Do we lose our temper when our battle comes? Do we lose our temper when things don't go according to the plan? Do we say one thing in church and live another out in the world? In prayer meetings we pray as though religion were the one thing needful. Are social ambition or money grabbing the chief end of our life outside the church walls?

Godly wisdom would say, "You had better be the same out in the world as you are in this church. We are the church lived out for the world. People don't come to church to see the building. They are out in the world and they saw something in the church that drew them in to see what really takes place.

The real issue is, when they get here, what do they see? What do they get? What do they go home and say?

If we walk through an orchard, pick up a fair-looking apple, and on biting into it find it sour, we throw it away. So too, the church is known by its fruit. Often people come into the church or into our lives and before they get out the door, it's like they've bitten into a bitter piece of fruit and said, "This is not for me."

It is imperative that we have good, Godly wisdom. There are those who are hurting, seeking for the answers to life. We say, "Come and experience the mighty power of God." But, do they receive something other than the power of God?

> Very few are made infidels by books that are evil or deadly, but many are made infidels by inconsistent Christians (Biblical Illustrator).

Proverbs 18:19 says,

> *A brother offended (is harder to be*
> *won) than a strong city: and (their)*
> *contentions [are] like the bars of a*
> *castle.*

When one person walks through the door of a church and leaves offended by something that happens, it means I could win the entire city before I could win that one back.

We need wisdom to know how to accept others, portray ourselves, and how to handle those in need that come to our churches. On the other hand, a noble, Godly life is a most convincing sermon. Often people are convinced not by what we say, but by how we live. You ought to preach every day of your life and when necessary, use words. You are to preach loudly by the way you handle yourself. That means when you are out in public, you had better live up to what you say in church.

THE SOURCE OF GODLY WISDOM

It is an absolute must that we seek the Lord for Godly wisdom. We can never win outsiders by compromising with them. The people of the world don't expect us to live as they do. When we surrender our principles, they are secretly disgusted. Many people think they have to make friends with the world to win the sinner. The problem is, sometimes we go to extremes.

While we think we are pleasing them and they are buying into our faith, they are secretly disgusted by what they see. We are supposed to be different.

To draw men out of the pit, we must have a strong foothold, a strong power, or they will draw us in with them. One of the things that destroys many leaders is that they go out before they are equipped, before they have dealt with the poison in their own lives. They go out before they have the goods. Ministry is tough. Ministry will have you celebrating at the end of the greatest sermon, but leave you devastated before you get out the door. The things people say will floor you, but wisdom says, "Don't worry about that."

As Christians, we have to be so rooted and grounded so when people want to slap us around, we can stand up under it. We may go home and cry like a baby, but when we are under the gun, we stand like men and women of faith and strength. We can stand tall as a child of God and say, "Hit me again, because in the Lord's name, I can take it."

The good news is, you are not known by what you say, as by what you do. An old preacher told me, "Boy, what you need to learn to do is let 99% of what you hear run off you like water off a duck's back." Wisdom will help you stand firm, stand solid, and be strong

Wisdom will make you look like you know something that no one else knows. I had rather be thought it fool and say nothing than to speak and remove all doubt. Wisdom would say, "It will be alright."

He who walks closest to Christ will have the most converting power through the Holy Spirit in one's life. We get close to Christ through prayer, fasting, and studying the Word. To walk in the Spirit and to be strong, you have to submit yourself to Godly teaching.

THE SOUL BUSINESS

We are in the soul business, and there isn't anything that requires more tact, more softness, more kind answers, and a more balanced approach than when we speak to a soul that is hurting. These are the people the world has beaten up. School has beaten them up. Their families have beaten them up. The job, life, and marriage have beaten them up. The last thing they need when they come to the house of God is to get beaten up again. People can get beat up just by the looks on our faces when they walk in the door. People are devastated by the poison in their lives.

If we want to water a flower, we do not pour a pail full over it, we sprinkle it.

God does not send His Holy Spirit as a waterspout, but as rain. Paul was consumed with zeal, yet showed wonderful wisdom and adaptation. He knew how to adapt to his surroundings. It is imperative that we know our surroundings. It is imperative that we know whom we are ministering to.

We are going to have to discover when there is a need without exposing that need in public. The word "need" is another way to say poison. We must find a way to minister to each individual a way to understand that with one person we can be very Pentecostal, while with another, we must be very gentle. When I minister to people, with some I may be really radical and with others, I take their hands and pray for them gently. Do you know why? I can hear the Spirit saying, "It is a major step for this individual to come and stand while you pray for them. The way they were raised, you didn't touch people. Where they were raised, everyone didn't pray at the same time. They serve the same God we serve, but where they come from, people didn't act this way." The Spirit would say through wisdom, "Every person has to be handled differently: the young, the old, the middle-aged, the single, the married. Every sect of life has to be handled with Godly wisdom."

This is one of the things we fight in the Pentecostal circle. Too many people think that if folks don't know how to worship the way we worship, it is their own fault. That is the attitude out there. Things are so different in Pentecostal churches that some people just can't connect with the way we do things. I believe that because of the lack of wisdom on our part, we sometimes lose potential members, great and faithful people.

If God called us, if God commissioned us, if God anointed us, and if God is truly in the house, then God wants to give us wisdom to reach the vast majority of people who come through our doors.

CREATING A TOTAL WORD MINISTRY

Our churches have to be a total Word ministry to minister to the total person: red, yellow, black or white, ugly, good-looking, rich, poor, retired, family man, single man or woman, sick or well person. Only Godly wisdom can give us the right mix. In Mark 10:14 we read,

But when Jesus sate (it), he was much displeased, and said unto them, Suffer the little children to come unto me, and forbid them not: for of such is the kingdom of God.

I think we can also refer to the ones who are hurting out in the world as the little children of God. He says to give up to what you think is right and give in to what God says will work (Mark 10:14, paraphrased). The only way we can do that is to walk into every service and say, "God, whatever you have for me, I am willing to accept."

The Bible mentions many occasions where Jesus held meetings, but it only talks about them having a shout one time: in the upper room. The rest of the time, He was teaching and preaching, loving, caring, and crying. So, if the Word is any indication as to how we are to live, we should follow Jesus' example. For every hundred times that Jesus spoke to the people, loved the people, and was there for the people, there was only one time when there was a shout (Acts 2). Wouldn't it be safe to say that it is important to be like Jesus? I don't know about you, but I feel God more in a setting where the Word is taught, than I do in the shout-and I am Pentecostal to the bone.

Wisdom would have us know and understand that God will speak into existence what He needs to happen. He doesn't need people to make things happen. Pushing your belief on someone else is sick. When I seek and talk about wisdom, and push my belief on someone else, it is sickening. We are to love, but not love too much. Over kill, kills.

RECOGNIZING GOD'S VOICE

I have been asked how I know if it is really God talking to me. First, let me say that your heart will be beating half out of your chest, because it will scare the life out of you. Second, whatever God is asking you to do, if it is a form of worship, it will never draw attention to you. If what you are about to do is going to draw attention to yourself, it is not God. When I am in the Spirit, the Spirit will allow me to flow as everyone is flowing and not create my own sideshow. I'll not out-sing anyone, I'll not out-preach anyone. I'll not step into an arena that is not my area of responsibility. In fact, the Word says, "Be still and know that I am God" (Psalms 46:10).

One of the reasons people in the Pentecostal movement don't know if it is God is because we Pentecostals don't know how to be still. I am talking about gaining wisdom. These tough lessons will make or break us. We must use and have Godly wisdom. Godly wisdom only comes from the teaching of the Word.

We do have freedom to worship, but God will never ask us to do anything that will override those who are over us in the Lord. God does not buck His system. God will not have you do something that is going to humiliate others.

Wisdom teaches us to watch for opportunities. It teaches us to redeem the time. We must seek out chances to put in the right word. When God sends the opportunity, we must make the most of it. We must operate on the now-or-never principle. We must, in our spirit, allow the Spirit of God to do the work. When God is at work, you don't always need a sermon. That is not the only way He moves. Sometimes He will move in a song or a testimony and that will be all the preaching that needs to happen.

No one likes to shout as much as I do. No one likes to whoop and holler like I do, but I don't feel that way every time I walk through the church doors. Wisdom says, when it is the Spirit, it will not offend or embarrass. Wisdom will never, ever cause you to do something that will embarrass you or the ministry.

Jesus came to eat with the publicans and sinners. He came to eat and spend time with those who were hurting. He didn't come and spend all His time with those who had it all figured out. He came to say that there are times we have to humble ourselves, especially whenever we minister to the souls of people.

You will never, ever see a fullness ministry as long as you have confusion in your services. The only thing that can stop chaos is that one word: wisdom. We should hug, but not over hug. We should sing, but not over-sing. We should have preaching, but not overpreach.

Ministers should always be listening to what they are saying, and how they are being perceived. Sometimes in the course of ministry and preaching, wisdom says, "Careful." Sometimes I stop in the middle of preaching, not because I've forgotten what I was saying, but because wisdom whispers, "Maybe you shouldn't say that." Wisdom will help us not to offend.

If we get to the place as Pentecostals where we think we are the answer, that is the first day of our death. We have to find a way to present the glorious gospel and help people understand what we are all about. God has helped me find the wisdom to pull together three books, but you will not find offensive pages in those books. It was settled in book one: my message is to the total, complete body of Christ. No matter what denomination a person is. If they read it, they are going to understand it.

Wisdom will cover a multitude of weaknesses. In all areas of ministry we must find wisdom. You don't have to defend yourself because you know who you are in the Lord. Ministry is not about any man, but it is all about Him. Wisdom will cause you to accomplish great and mighty things for Him.

James 1:1-8 says,

> *James, a servant of God and of the Lord Jesus Christ, to the twelve tribes which are scattered abroad, greetings. My brethren, count it all joy when ye fall into divers temptations; Knowing this, that the trying of your faith worketh patience. But let patience have her perfect work, that ye may be perfect and entire, wanting nothing. If any of you lack wisdom, let him ask of God, that giveth to all men liberally, and upbraideth not; and it shall be given him. But let him ask in faith, nothing wavering. For he that wavereth is like a wave of the sea driven with the wind and is tossed. For let not that man think that he shall receive any thing of the Lord. A double minded man is unstable in all his ways.*

This simply tells us that if we lack wisdom, we can ask the Lord and He will give it to us. In dealing with the poison in our lives it is imperative that we ask the Lord to help us avoid being double-minded. We can't believe in the ways of the world one day and the next believe in the ways of God's Holy Word.

Seek the Lord concerning the poison in your life and ask Him for wisdom in knowing what to do. He can and will clean the poison out of your life.

Bibliography

1. Nelson's New Illustrated Bible Dictionary, Copyright 1995, 1996, Thomas Nelson Publishers.
2. The Biblical Illustrator, by Joseph S. Exell, Copyright 1973, Baker Book House Grand Rapids, Michigan.
3. The NIV Matthew Henry Commentary in One Volume, Copyright 1992, Zondervan Publishing House, Grand Rapids, Michigan.
4. Holman Bible Dictionary, Copyright 1991, Holman Bible Publishers, Nashville, Tennessee.
5. The Thompson Chain Reference Bible, Copyright 1988, B. B. Kirkbride Bible Company, Inc., Indianapolis, Indiana.
6. Webster's Universal Dictionary, Copyright 1936, The World Syndicate Publishing, Co., New York.

About the Author

Don R Vining is a dedicated minister and seasoned entrepreneur, bringing over forty-five years of experience to both ministry and business. Throughout his life, Don has played a key role in planting new churches, passionately advancing the Kingdom of God through leadership, mentorship, and faithful service.

Don completed the Ministerial Internship Program under the recommendation of the State Board of Education of the Church of God. He holds ministerial credentials as an Exhorter, Licensed Minister, and Ordained Bishop with the Church of God, headquartered in Cleveland, Tennessee. In 2017, he was recognized for twenty-five years of service as a credentialed minister.

In 2002, Don was awarded an Honorary Doctor of Ministry degree from Jacksonville Theological Seminary, a recognition of his lifelong commitment to spiritual growth, leadership, and the equipping of the saints.

A devoted husband and father, Don resides in Belleview, Florida. His life and ministry are marked by a deep passion for Christ and a sincere desire to help others grow in faith through the power of spiritual understanding and transformation. His journey reflects a calling to serve, to teach, and to walk alongside others as they discover God's purpose for their lives.